THE
GOLF
record system

THE
GOLF
record system

NEIL-MONTICELLI HARLEY-RUDD

RUNNING PRESS
PHILADELPHIA · LONDON

First published in the United States in 2009 by
Running Press Book Publishers

Printed in China

9   8   7   6   5   4   3   2   1
Digit on the right indicates the number
of this printing

Library of Congress Control Number: 2008939352

ISBN 978-0-7624-3655-2

This book and disc was conceived, designed,
and produced by:
ILEX, Cambridge, England

Running Press Book Publishers
2300 Chestnut Street
Philadelphia, PA 19103-4371

Visit us on the web!
www.runningpress.com

Contents

PLAYING THE GAME

SCORING

USING THE GOLF RECORD SYSTEM

TOP COURSES

INTRODUCTION

Millions of people across the globe regularly play golf, either competitively or socially, which is hardly surprising as it's possibly one of the oldest sports in the world. Variants of stick-and-ball games can be traced back as far as Julius Caesar and as far away as China, where the game *Chuiwan* ("ball hitting") was documented in the 11th Century.

The modern game, however, is believed to have originated in either the Netherlands or Scotland (depending on your train of thought or romantic notion). A sport similar to modern day golf was played during medieval times in Holland, where the game was known locally as *spel metten colven* ("game played with club").

It is Scotland though, that many people now accept as the birthplace of the modern game, with words such as *golff*, *golve*, *gouf*, and *gowf* all possibly having referred to the game in the past. Elderly patriotic Scottish golfers still sometimes use the latter term, and The Royal & Ancient Golf Club (R&A) at St. Andrews in Fife, Scotland, is now universally recognized as the "home of golf."

The first written reference to golf matches at St. Andrews dates back to 1552, when Archbishop

Hamilton's Charter reserved the right of the people of St. Andrews to use the links-land "for golff, futball, schuteing, and all gamis." It has not always been a popular past-time though, and three Scottish kings—James II in 1457, James III in 1471, and James IV in 1491—banned the sport because they believed people were spending too much time playing golf and not devoting enough time to practicing their archery skills.

This changed when King James VI of Scotland (later King James I of England) became fascinated by the sport in the 17th century, which is where the royal connection in the Royal & Ancient's name derived from.

Steeped in history, the R&A has a Rules Committee that imposes and oversees the official rules of the game, in conjunction with the United States Golf Association (USGA). These rules are used internationally by both amateurs and professionals, and it is the R&A that was responsible for introducing 18-hole golf courses in 1858, even though this meant it had to merge some of its holes to reduce its course to 18 holes.

The first 18-hole course to appear in North America came almost 35 years later when, in 1892, Charles Blair Macdonald, who had been to college in Scotland where he learned the game, built a 9-hole course on land in Wheaton, Illinois. The following year Macdonald doubled the number of holes at the Chicago Golf Club, and with four other golf clubs laid the foundations for the United States Golf Association which was founded in 1894.

Yet while Macdonald got the ball rolling with the USGA, it was a British golfer—Harry Vardon (pictured below)—who popularized the sport in the United States In 1900, Vardon—the only 6-time winner of the British Open—took his game across the Atlantic, playing over 80 exhibition matches (of which he won more than 70) and winning the US Open. Vardon became the first international golf "celebrity," paving the way for a game that now sees 36.7 million golfers play 500 million rounds of golf per year across the USA.

As a result of its popularity, golf has evolved into a lucrative business for all involved, especially for the winner of the annual Nedbank Golf Challenge competition in Sun City, South Africa, where the prize is a cool US$1.2 million.

Yet regardless of whether you're a seasoned pro, or a keen amateur, every golfer has special memories of matches played. With *The Golf Record System* you can make sure that all of your rounds are recorded, providing you with a unique testimony to your best (and worst) moments on the golf course.

What makes the game of golf such an attractive participation sport is its diversity, which allows players to strategically tackle the course's terrain while avoiding natural and man-made hazards. Although most courses contain the same features—18 holes with tees leading onto fairways, with each hole positioned on a beautifully manicured green—the course design and terrain, as well as the weather conditions, determine the varying degrees of difficulty.

Modern-day golf course architects appear to have reverted back to the 19th century concept of letting nature decide the course's overall design, with newer courses having a tendency to look and feel as though the terrain had always existed as the most perfect setting for a golf course.

With around 30,000 rounds of golf a year racked up on each course around the world, it is important for the designers to provide a challenge for players so they want to return to tackle the course again and again. One way of doing this is to encourage players to try and use most of their golf clubs over a round, making the game more tactical and generating genuine excitement for the players.

On The Course

DESIGN & MAINTENANCE

As nature intended

The main objective of a modern day golf course architect is to design the course in keeping with its surroundings, so the manmade course and natural terrain exist in harmony. Golf courses also play an important role in the environment, especially in the United States where such sporting arenas provide a buffer between fully urbanized areas and undeveloped land.

Sheep shelters create hazards

The original game of golf was played on unkempt land that was only fit for grazing sheep. In Scotland that meant links-land, with rugged courses built on barren coasts where North Sea winds viciously swept in to create a mysterious ambiance.

It was the sheep that introduced bunkers, quite by chance, as they huddled together to escape the cold wind and rubbed themselves in the sandy soil.

In doing so, the first golf course hazards were introduced, and the placement of bunkers is now considered a skill, rather than a natural occurrence, with top designers having mastered this art down to a tee.

12

WORLD'S TRICKIEST PAR THREE

Building a new golf course—complete with practice facilities and a clubhouse—requires around 300 acres of land, with most courses starting and ending at the clubhouse

Unsurprisingly, Scotland, the undisputed "home to golf," boasts the world's most copied golf hole. Despite being built in 1832, the 15th hole on the West Links course at North Berwick has been recreated globally. Known as the "Redan Hole," this par three is set with the green diagonal to the direction of the tee shot, with a hazard guarding the left side of the green.

The Augusta National's 12th hole, known as the "Golden Bell," is comparable to the Redan Hole and is considered to be the world's most difficult tournament par three.

13

Just an illusion

Creating a golf course means providing numerous challenges and delivering a rewarding experience for players. Hazards force golfers to think strategically before striking the ball, and a leading designer will have excelled with his creation if golfers get the opportunity to use virtually all 14 clubs in their bag.

Ideally, a course needs to appear lenient to players and combine a variety of hole lengths. In addition, it needs to be visually pleasing, and this is often achieved when the designer works to enhance the land's natural characteristics, rather than create a completely artificial setting.

Reshaping land

Rapid technological advances in the equipment used to maintain golf courses has resulted in an ever-increasing number of immaculately sculpted fairways. Contour mowing means fairways can be precisely sculpted, while the ability to reshape the land is used to adjust their size.

Early courses used to play both "out" and "in" over a straight line, which resulted in players only having to adjust their game to the wind from two directions, but modern designers favor a looping design for greater variety, so the 18 holes can be tackled from various directions.

Aesthetically pleasing

The priority of maintenance is to offer a golf course that permits players to enjoy the pleasure of regular rounds of golf. The greens receive the most attention, as golfers congregate on these precisely-trimmed putting surfaces. In today's environmentally-friendly era, golf courses are designed and remodeled to fit in with the harmony of the land to ensure long-term benefits to the environment and wildlife. Modern golf holes need to be aesthetically pleasing rather than solely designed for the purpose of playing golf, although a happy medium needs to be found in the search for perfection.

WHAT APPEARS ON A GOLF COURSE

Tackling tricky terrain

Golf courses generally consist of 18 holes, although many prestigious clubs boast three or more 18 hole courses, and nine hole courses are more common in Europe. Golf courses consist of three main sections—the tee, the fairway, and the green—which offer varying challenges and encourage players to try different clubs for each hole. Golfers start at the tee and aim to keep the ball confined to the fairway, but face elements of danger before reaching the green.

Don't be teed off by color coding

The tee—also referred to as the tee-box and the teeing area—is where players take their first shot to start the hole. This is known as teeing off. The objective is to hit the ball safely onto the fairway (or green), and as close to the flagstick on the green as possible. Rules stipulate that teeing off takes place between two markers and players can take their first shot from up to two club lengths behind, but never in front of these marks.

Different colored markers are used to indicate the teeing area, depending on who is playing, although there is no universal standard as to which colors must be used and what they mean.

Throughout Europe, three main colors signify the teeing area; white (used for men's competitions); yellow (men's friendlies), and red (ladies, juniors, and beginners).

In the United States, the colors are; black (men's competitions); blue (high handicaps); white (men's friendlies); red (ladies, juniors, and beginners); yellow (senior men); silver (senior women), and green (novices).

Stake your fairway to heaven

The fairway is the area of the hole that comprises well-maintained short grass and a range of hazards to challenge players. From the tee shot, golf balls usually land on the fairway—in the center for safety.

Stakes in the middle of the fairway show the distance to the center of the green; blue indicates it is 200 yards (183 m) away, white is 150 yards (137 m), and red means the ball lies 100 yards (91.5 m) from the center of the green.

There are also stakes to indicate boundaries: green (environmentally sensitive area), red (lateral water hazard), white (ground under repair or out of bounds), and yellow (water hazard).

Avoid the rough stuff

The rough is the area of the course that lines the fairway. It consists of longer grass than the fairways and greens, and is usually made up of shrubland, thick grass, and woodland. Although it isn't maintained like the fairways and greens, the rough is still an very important part of a golf course, acting as a natural hazard that is tricky to play out of and punishing poor shots.

Keep out, or pay the penalty

Out of bounds is an area that is clearly marked—usually by wooden fences or stakes—as being outside the confines of the golf course. If any portion of the ball lies out of bounds, penalty strokes are applied, although how many depends on the match format.

Touch of drama

Hazards have many uses, inviting golfers to strategically ponder how to tackle the course and adding a touch of drama to the game. The main hazard on a hole is a bunker containing sand, normally located on the edge of the putting green. These can confound the majority of golfers, although more experienced players will have learnt how to recover should they fail to fly over, or play around, the bunkers.

Other hazards include natural elements such as creeks, lakes, ponds, and streams, with penalty strokes applied if you fail to avoid them and end up with a lost ball.

Pin your hopes on the green

The green has the smoothest surface on the entire course, with the "grain" (the growth direction of the blades of grass) and the slope of the surface affecting the roll of the ball.

The green is also where players find their ultimate goal—the hole. The aim of golf is to putt the ball down the hole (referred to as the "cup"), which must have a minimum diameter of 4.25 inches (108 mm) and a depth of at least 3.94 inches (100 mm)

The cup's position is not fixed, and is often changed due to wear and tear. However, it must lie at least 10 feet (approx. 3 m) from the edge of the green, and a flagstick is placed in the hole to indicate the final target from a distance. The color of the flag indicates to a distant golfer where the hole has been cut that day and there are generally three different colored flags; blue (meaning the hole has been cut at the back of the green); white (middle of the green), and red (front of the green).

LEADING DESIGNERS

Eco-friendly layouts

As an industry, golf—like many other sports—has welcomed changes brought about by high-profile environmental awareness and is benefiting from effective land use.

Big name players still plying their trade on the PGA Tour, such as Phil Mickleson and Tiger Woods, are also now cashing in as course designers, designing exclusive courses based on their playing experience

Distinctive good looks

Golf course architects have always been respected for their achievements, but the modern era has seen a handful of the top designers recognized for producing some of the world's most spectacular manmade scenery. What makes courses in the United States so distinctive is that they are enticingly long and good-looking, with plenty of space devoted to them. Starting in the late 1940s, Robert Trent Jones, Sr. was responsible for championing this spacious style, along with modern designers such as George Cobb, George & Tom Fazio, Joe Lee, and Dick Wilson.

Scottish influences

Leading golf course architect Pete Dye started a new trend in the 1960s, which remains as popular today as it did almost 50 years ago. Dye's trademark designs were inspired by a trip to see Scotland's rugged courses first-hand, and on his return to the United States he concentrated on bringing the natural world and course design together. His concept was to create courses that looked as natural as they could—courtesy of the lie of the land, natural hazards, and tight fairways.

Dr Alistair McKenzie

*Robert Trent Jones,
Sr. (left) and Jr. (right)*

Jack Nicklaus

The rationale behind his unique creations was to give the impression that the course was a simple tweak of the land supplied by Mother Nature.

Great golfers create challenges

Modern era golfers like Jack Nicklaus, Greg Norman, Arnold Palmer, Gary Player, and Lee Trevino have received many accolades over the years for their ability as leading golf course designers. With a natural flair, they can individually inject their vast experience to create challenges from a truly great golfer's perspective. The results are a marvel, with the fabulous course creations boasting complex hazards and hole designs to stretch players of all standards.

A BRIEF HISTORY OF COURSE DESIGN

Pre-1899 As moving land was out of the question, it was nature that provided the designs. Course creators spent only a couple of days on site to stake out the greens and tees, with only a handful of decisions to make.

1900-1948 Architects were given a free hand to introduce hazards for both aesthetic and strategic reasons, which ensured golfers got maximum enjoyment from courses offering varying levels of difficulty. This was brought across the Atlantic Ocean to the United States by designers such as Charles Blair Macdonald before the "Golden Age" of course creations in the 1920s.

1949-1985 Robert Trent Jones, Sr. started a trend with the United States' now distinct designs, basing his creations on length and looks. In the 1960s, Pete Dye was responsible for turning the tide away from bland courses after visits to Scottish courses inspired him to create courses with a more rugged look and feel..

1986-to date Visual impact was the priority for courses in the late '80s, although many of the manufactured courses were not particularly challenging. Towards the end of the century, designers returned to the roots of the original designs by appreciating the existing terrain and utilizing nature to create the perfect course.

21

GOLF COURSE STYLES

Links

Links courses are the most traditional type of golf course, dating back to the origins of the modern game. They are built on land that has been reclaimed from the sea, with beaches forming the few water hazards and sandy soil featuring natural bunkers and a sprinkling of trees.

The world's most famous links course is The Old Course at St. Andrews in Scotland, a country that is home to some of the finest examples of links courses that date back to the 1800s.

Parkland

These courses are typically located inland and resemble the romantic notion of traditional parks. Neatly manicured, lawn-like fairways lead on to short-trimmed greens, with both picturesquely surrounded by established trees and wildlife.

Heathland

This style is also commonly found inland, and mainly features naturally occurring gorse bushes and heather. These courses are not over-manicured as they lie relatively open and are not protected from the elements by trees. Gleneagles in Scotland is arguably the world's best-known heathland course.

Snow

Although the game of golf can be played in the snow around the globe, genuine snow courses are only commonplace in the Arctic or sub-Arctic regions during the coldest times of the year. Designated courses comprising snow are relatively new, with sleighs replacing golf carts and the use of highly visible golf balls a necessity. The "19th hole" is also a real must, in order to warm up from the experience of playing a round of golf in freezing temperatures.

Desert and sand

A modern and popular creation, this style of course can only be tackled in the world's driest climes—such as Australia, the Middle East, and in some areas of the United States. Because of the existing landscape, desert courses vary, but environmentalists criticize their heavy use of irrigation, especially in times of drought.

A more eco-friendly option—and one that gives golfers a unique experience—is playing on a sand course, as their "greens" are not as heavily irrigated.

GOLF COURSE TYPES

Despite every golf course having a similar structure of tees, fairways, bunkers, and greens, no two courses are the same, so golfers face a unique challenge wherever they play. Amenities, prices, and maintenance are the main differences between private and public courses.

Public

A public course is the cheapest way to start playing golf, although they do not always offer a full complement of 18 holes—you may have to play nine holes twice to complete a round. Mainly situated in urban areas, public courses are run as a business first and foremost, so they may not be as neatly manicured as you might expect. You will need to check in advance whether you can just turn up and play during the week—many public courses allow this—but to avoid disappointment it is advisable to book a tee time if you want to play at the weekend or on public holidays.

Advantage: Cheap and available
Disadvantage: Too easy

Municipal

Municipal courses are very similar to public golf courses in that they are run as a business, are excellent value, and the game can be played at a leisurely pace. The main difference is that municipal golf courses exist for the benefit of local residents. Non-resident golfers can still play a round, although they will be expected to pay slightly more to do so.

Advantage: Inexpensive
Disadvantage: Not challenging

Semi-private

Expect to pay slightly more money to play a round at a semi-private course compared to public and municipal courses. Golfers pay a daily fee, but should book a tee time in advance and be aware that there are likely to be restrictions on when you can play because of corporate events and tournaments. As there is usually a membership facility, this type of course is suitable for golfers who want a sense of belonging to a golf club and also enjoy the social amenities.

Advantage: Good quality
Disadvantage: Availability

Resort

With tourism booming, high-class hotels now boast spectacular, world-class courses that have often been designed by former professional players. They are generally available to the resort's guests as an amenity, to encourage them to book their vacation with them. Non-paying guests are usually welcome, although a few charge outrageous prices.

Advantage: Stunning
Disadvantage: Remote location

Private

These elite courses are members-only clubs for those with sufficient time and funds. The annual fees make them the most expensive type of golf course to play on, but for your money you can expect finely groomed fairways, precisely cut teeing areas, and manicured greens, along with the exclusivity. They are frequently known as country clubs.

Advantage: Pampered
Disadvantage: Expensive

The private 18-hole golf course of The Royal Bangkok Sports Club, Thailand

TEE TIMES & GREEN FEES

Recent leaps in modern technology mean there are now specialist online services where you can conveniently browse and book tee times and pay your golf green fees at whichever course you fancy a challenge. Your confirmation is immediate, with bookings available up to 180 days in advance. For last minute availability there are also specialist websites. Alternatively you can directly book over the telephone, or in person, with the course of your choice.

Booking tee times

Tee times can be booked in advance at the golf course, either in person or by telephone, or online. To ensure a suitable tee time it is advisable to book after your playing partner(s) have confirmed their availability.

Canceling tee times

One of the playing partners booked for the predetermined tee time is responsible for contacting the golf course to notify them of any cancellation. If possible, try to give at least 24 hours notice. If you continually fail to turn up without informing the course, you may be penalized or refused future tee times.

Paying green fees

All playing parties should aim to arrive at least 30 minutes before the tee time. Once all players are gathered at the course, you are collectively expected to check in and pay your green fee. By arriving early you can warm-up by practicing your swing or trying out the putting practice area.

GOLF ATTIRE

Dress for success

It is imperative to dress appropriately for a round of golf, and jeans and T-shirts are definitely frowned upon, even if it is a designer label! But what is widely acceptable? Obviously it depends where you are playing, and with whom, but most private golf courses have a standardized dress code of a golf shirt with a collar, and golf shorts or slacks with belt loops. It is also a good idea to have a golf jacket, sweater, and vest in your bag.

Color coordinate

As golf attire is generally colorful and patterned, opt to wear one brightly colored top paired with neutral slacks. A classic combination of blue or brown with khaki is appropriate for less daring dressers, and one pattern per outfit is advisable.

Feet first

Golf shoes are the only footwear allowed on the course. Metal spikes are deemed a little bit old-fashioned, with soft spikes or built-in spikes now more acceptable. Smart street shoes cannot be used on the courses, but should be worn to the club and in the bar/restaurant. Never change into your golf shoes in the parking lot—use the locker room instead.

Socks appeal

If you opt for slacks, ensure that the color of your socks matches them. If you are wearing shorts, black shoes without socks is acceptable. Otherwise match black socks and shoes together, or combine light colored socks with white shoes.

Hats all folks

Hats are a useful accessory, ensuring you are warm on colder days, or the sun is kept out of your eyes. Baseball style hats (not back-to-front!) or specialist straw golf hats are ideal in the summer, while a sensible wool hat is most appropriate in the cold.

ETIQUETTE

Spirit of the game

As the game of golf is generally played without a referee or umpire, players are expected to use common sense to compete fairly in the spirit of the game and keep an accurate score. Therefore, proper etiquette—care, courtesy, and priority on the course—plays an important role.

There are no specific rules attached to etiquette, although the official *Rules of Golf* from the Royal & Ancient has a section devoted to it. The R&A points out that for the majority of players, "golf is a cherished hobby used as a means of escaping the stresses of everyday life." So, distracting a player when they are about to make a stroke is one major faux pas, and others can range from innocently casting your shadow over an opponent's ball to talking on a cell phone. The number one rule is to be considerate to others, not just your opponents.

On the course

Order of play: The player with the lowest handicap is first to tee off at the start, with the winner of the previous hole having the honor of teeing off on subsequent holes. After the tee shots, the golfer whose ball is furthest from the hole plays first, with the next nearest player going second, and so forth.

Teeing off: Pick up your tee after your shot (even if you have broken it) and wait for others to take their turn.

Fairways: Repair divots by replacing the grass chunks and pushing them back into place.

Bunkers: Enter the bunker, rake in hand, from the low side nearest your ball. Cover your tracks by raking the sand after your shot and leave the rake outside the bunker with the handle running parallel to the fairway.

Greens: As with the general order of play, the first golfer to putt is the one furthest away from the hole, with the second furthest ball played next, and so on.

After a missed putt, if your ball is within two feet (60 cm) of the hole you have the option to "putt out" (to complete the hole), or mark behind your ball. When others are putting, ensure that you—and your shadow—are not encroaching on an opponent's line. As hitting the flagstick results in a penalty stroke, one person needs to hold the flagstick by the flag and lift it out before the ball reaches the hole.

On greens, NEVER:
- Place your bag of clubs on the green
- Step on the putting line where an opponent's ball could travel
- Remove the flagstick from the hole until all players are on the green (unless requested)
- Throw the flagstick, or leave it on the green after it has been removed from the hole

Scoring: You should fill in your scorecard when you reach the next teeing area, not on the green.

Lost ball: You are expected to spend up to five minutes helping opponents search for a lost ball. If it is not found, a new ball is dropped where it was expected to be and a penalty stroke is added.

GOOD MANNERS

Keeping Quiet: On the teeing area and greens, silence must be kept while golfers are poised to play their shots. Keep your voice down on fairways, as you are not the only players on the course.

Shouting: If your shot has any likelihood of hitting anyone on the course, yell "fore" to warn them of the danger of a stray ball.

Pacing Play: Always wait until players in the game ahead of you are out of the way before hitting your shot. It is acceptable to invite faster groups behind yours to play ahead of you.

Golf Carts: Stay on the cart path as much as possible, and never drive golf carts near the teeing areas and greens.

Golf equipment has developed from simple handmade clubs and wooden balls, to today's kit, which utilizes computer-aided design and materials such as titanium and diamonds.

According to *The Rules of Golf*, golfers are permitted to carry up to 14 clubs in their bag during a round of golf, with each club distinguishable by its length, shape, and size. The R&A and the USGA update the rules annually to maintain fair competitiveness. For example, on January 1, 2008, the ruling authorities had to limit the so-called "trampoline effect" of a recently designed wood, which they felt offered players an unfair advantage.

Balls are also subject to *The Rules of Golf* and, like clubs, they have seen radical changes throughout golf's history. The best-known early ball is the "Featherie," which was often more expensive than a club due to its goose feather filling and hand-stitched leather exterior. The high cost of equipment meant that from the 1600s to mid-1850s golf was seen as an "elitist" sport, played only by those with both leisure time and money.

However, this all changed when the Featherie was superseded by the much cheaper, mass-produced, smooth "Guttie" ball. Golf promptly became more accessible, and wooden-headed clubs also began to be mass-produced, increasing the numbers of players able to get involved in the game.

Equipment

GOLF BALLS

History of the golf ball

In the earliest documented existence of golf, players used wooden balls, which were replaced in 1618 with the introduction of the "Featherie" golf ball. These handcrafted balls were fashioned from a mass of goose feathers packed into cow or horse leather, and shaped while wet. As the feathers dried and expanded, they helped to create a hard ball that was then painted and punched by the ball maker's individual stamp. The most famous ball makers at the time were the St. Andrews' outfit of Andrew Dickson and Henry Mills. These handmade works of art proved to be very expensive, but this didn't stop affluent players from drilling holes in them and adding lead shot to weigh them down to cope with blustery weather conditions.

Guttie balls

The game was brought to the general public in 1848, with the invention of the "Guttie" golf ball by Reverend Adam Paterson of St. Andrews. The Guttie ball was so named because it was made by heating the rubber-like sap of tropical Gutta trees (common in Malaysia), and shaping it into a small spherical shape to be used as a golf ball. These were relatively cheap to produce, and as the material could be reheated they could easily be reshaped or repaired.

The only drawbacks were that they failed to travel as far as the Featheries, and had a tendency to shatter. In attempts to increase their travel distance, Gutties started to adopt various surface patterns from 1881, and in 1890 the creation of the popular "Bramble" design—raised spherical bumps on the surface—resulted in the balls being made in moulds to improve their quality. Dunlop was one of many rubber companies that killed off the handmade ball business with their own mass-produced golf balls.

Haskell's invention is a big hit

In 1898, Coburn Haskell introduced the one-piece, rubber-cored ball, which was universally adopted after it helped Alex Herd win The Open in 1902. This ball—identical in appearance to the Gutties—added at least an extra 20 yards (18 m) from tee shots, and allowed golfers much more control and spin.

As a result, The Open in 1903 witnessed almost every player using the same ball that had been a big hit for Herd the previous year. These balls were constructed from a solid rubber core, wrapped in rubber thread, and encased in a "Gutta Percha" sphere.

After the development of W. Millison's thread winding machine, these "Haskell" golf balls were soon mass-produced. In 1905, William Taylor introduced the dimple pattern to minimize drag and maximize lift. It was this design that acted as the fore-runner to the dimpling that is seen on modern golf balls.

Haskell's original one-piece design was not replaced until 1968, when Spalding introduced the inaugural two-piece ball named "The Executive." It is the most consistent golf ball and stays "in round" and "in play" far longer than softer balata-covered balls.

Timeline of the Golf Ball

1550	John Daly plays with a wooden golf ball in Scotland
1618	First "Featherie" golf ball appears, created out of goose feathers, leather, and paint
1848	St. Andrews' Reverend Adam Paterson introduces the "Guttie" or "Gutta Percha" golf ball
1881	Patterns appear on the outside of Guttie golf balls in a bid to make them travel further
1880s	Bramble pattern used on Guttie golf balls
1890	Guttie golf balls made out of moulds to improve quality
1890s	Dunlop leads the number of rubber companies that are mass-producing golf balls
1898	Coburn Haskell invents one-piece, rubber-cored golf ball
1902	Alex Herd wins The Open using one-piece, rubber-cored golf ball, at Hoylake, England
1905	William Taylor's dimple pattern on wound-rubber golf balls is a big hit
1906	Goodrich's pneumatic golf ball introduced but explodes when too hot
1921	The R&A Rules specify ball characteristics of 1.62 inch (41.15 mm) and 1.62oz (45.93 g)
1922	The USGA introduces experimental 1.7-inch (43.18 mm) diameter golf ball
1929	The USGA adopts a 1.68-inch (42.67 mm), 1.55oz (43.94 g) golf ball for 1930-31
1932	The USGA specifies golf ball characteristics of 1.68 inch (42.7 mm), 1.62oz (45.93 g)
1964	The PGA makes 1.68-inch (42.67 mm) golf balls compulsory for main tournaments
1968	The PGA makes 1.68-inch (42.67 mm) golf balls compulsory for all tournaments. Spalding introduces a two-piece ball, called "The Executive"
1974	The R&A makes 1.68-inch (42.67 mm) golf balls compulsory for the Open Championship
1976	The R&A imposes a limit on the velocity a golf ball may have at impact
1984	The R&A imposes a limit on the overall distance standard of a golf ball
1990	The R&A bans golf balls smaller than 1.68 inches (42.67 mm)

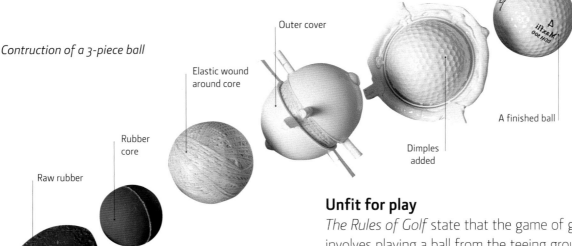

Contruction of a 3-piece ball

Outer cover

Elastic wound around core

Rubber core

Raw rubber

Dimples added

A finished ball

Size matters

Golf ball specifications for size, weight, spherical symmetry, an overall distance standard, and initial velocity are set in *The Rules of Golf*. On a monthly basis, the USGA publishes and updates a "List of Conforming Golf Balls" that are permitted for use in competitions, and there are currently just under 900 different balls that conform.

The current regulations require a golf ball to have a diameter that is no less than 1.68 inches (42.67 mm), weigh no more than 1.62 oz (45.93 g), possess spherical symmetry, be able to travel an overall distance no greater than 296.8 yards (271.4 m), with an initial velocity no greater than 255 feet per second (279.8 km/h) when measured on apparatus approved by the USGA.

Some recent models of balls have been introduced to the game that conform to these rules, despite being around 2% larger than ordinary balls. Their softer cores and thicker covers help produce longer and straighter shots.

Unfit for play

The Rules of Golf state that the game of golf involves playing a ball from the teeing ground into the hole, establishing the general principle that a player may not change his or her ball while playing a hole. However, this is only prohibited under competition conditions, as there are situations where it is impossible to use the same ball— such as when a ball is lost, or shatters.

If the ball becomes "unfit for play" it can be substituted, and being "unfit for play" refers to the original ball being visibly cut, cracked, or out-of-shape. If you suspect your ball has become unfit for play, it must be announced before lifting it to inspect, and you have to give your opponent an opportunity to examine it. Failure to follow this procedure incurs a one-stroke penalty. The ball cannot be cleaned when it is lifted if it is not deemed "unfit for play" and has to be returned to the position that you marked.

Simply falling apart

Although it's not that common, golf balls can shatter as a result of a normal stroke. If this happens, the stroke is immediately cancelled, and the golfer has to use a substitute ball from the same spot. This rule first appeared in the mid-19th century as Gutta Percha balls, having recently replaced feather balls, often broke into pieces. The rule meant that the golfer could substitute another ball at the place where the largest portion of the original ball ended up.

The R&A altered this rule in 1908, declaring that another ball could be dropped where any of the broken pieces lay, not just the largest part.

When the wound, three-piece ball was introduced in the early 20th century, there were no such problems, to the point that from 1933 there was no mention in the rules of balls breaking. However, the rule was reinstated in 1976 because the solid-core balls that had become popular would occasionally split, or break into pieces.

WHAT BALLS ARE MADE OF

COVER MATERIAL

Balata

Soft material for feel and control, so not as long-lasting as other materials

Elastomer

Favored by experts who seek spin without losing durability

Surlyn

As the cheapest and most durable material it is found on the majority of golf balls

CORES

Wound

Ideal for spin rather than distance, characteristics influenced by the combination of the core and cover material. The core—liquid or solid—is wound around with a rubber thread and coated.

Advantage – Spin

Disadvantage – Less Durability

Two-piece

Ideal for height rather than control, by being so hard the result is a high take-off angle leading to less carry. The core is made of a resin type material and the cover is surlyn.

Advantage – Durability

Disadvantage – Less Distance

Three-piece

Ideal for serious players, with a flatter take-off angle and ultimately a higher trajectory. It is made of a large synthetic core, a thin mantel, and a coat.

Advantage – Distance

Disadvantage – Sideways spin

Four-piece

Ideal for those seeking long distance drives. The small inner core is surrounded by a thin inner mantel that transmits relevant distance characteristics, which is within another core and a coat.

Advantage – Distance

Disadvantage – Expensive

CHOOSING A GOLF CLUB

Materials

Stainless steel

Stainless steel is the most commonly used material in golf as it is generally inexpensive, easy to cast into all golf club shapes, and is durable enough for everyday play.

Two main grades of stainless steel are used in golf club heads; 17-4 for irons, and 431 for putters. The 17-4 grade is made up of 75% iron and trace elements, 15–17% chromium, and 4% nickel, whereas 431 includes no more than 20% carbon, 15–17% chromium, 1.25–2.5% nickel, with iron and trace elements making up the remaining materials.

Advantage: Durable
Disadvantage: Heavy

Maraging steel

This premium-priced, speciality stainless steel is mainly used for golf face inserts rather than the whole head of a club, as it is a strong, high performance material.

Advantage: Strength
Disadvantage: Expensive

Carbon graphite

Carbon graphite is the least dense material used for golf clubs, but it commands high prices. Very few clubs—except drivers—are made out of carbon graphite; instead it is used primarily as a weight-saving material in the crown of a club, allowing additional weight to be repositioned in the club head.

Advantage: Light
Disadvantage: Expensive

Aluminum

Experimental club designs in the 1970s and 1980s saw cheap, mass-produced aluminum club heads appear on golf courses worldwide, but as the lightweight material is neither durable nor strong, players' shiny new clubs quickly became scuffed and scratched. Modern clubs with aluminum alloys are more durable than the early prototypes, and the low cost allows drivers' heads to be designed to the maximum permitted size.

Advantage: Affordable
Disadvantage: Durability

Titanium

Originating from the aerospace industry, titanium golf clubs rocketed to success after titanium drivers began to appear in the early 1990s. The space-age material is extremely light, yet powerful, resulting in large club heads boasting a high strength-to-weight ratio. Varying degrees of titanium alloys are used, but the high cost factor means it is primarily used as a driver, although many golfers benefit from playing with titanium irons.

Advantage: Strength
Disadvantage: Expensive

Zinc

Economical, both financially and in terms of weight, zinc heads are a popular choice for beginners who benefit from the enhanced sweet spot.

Advantage: Inexpensive
Disadvantage: Durability

Wood

Traditional wooden club heads are becoming rare, as they are superseded by a slew of technological breakthroughs and more cost-effective materials.

Advantage: Strong
Disadvantage: Out-of-date

Grips

Because golf grips are the least expensive part of a golf club, they are often overlooked, despite playing an integral role in how polished a player's game is. There are a number of official rules relating to grips, but from an individual's point of view the golden rule is to change your golf club grips after about 3,000 rounds. The highest quality grips have a tendency to lose their feel quickest, and signs of requiring an upgrade are when the grips harden, get slick, or oxidize. It is advisable to calculate how much you will benefit from superior grips in comparison to the longevity factor.

Invest in the best

It is literally a jungle out there when investing in golf clubs, with manufacturers bombarding golfers with endless (and often justifiable) reasons why they should opt for their brand—for example, Diamond Touch actually use diamonds to ensure its club heads are incredibly solid and eliminate spin. The specialty strengths of some of the world's most marketed golf brands is useful to know, although it is recommended that you ask about suitability prior to purchase as most manufacturers generally produce excellent game-improvement clubs.

Clubs: WOODS

With club heads now available as oversized and square, modern woods—with their dense and heavy heads—are a far cry from the traditional club. Originally, woods had a thick hosel to provide a secure join between the shaft and head, but the introduction of various metals in the 1970s means manufacturers no longer require a hosel as they have anchored the shaft within the club head to lower the center of gravity.

Toward the end of the last century, the R&A and the USGA introduced a size rule on woods to prevent the rapid volumetric growth of clubs spiraling out of control. This rule was made to curb what was arguably the most successful modern-era series of clubs—Callaway Golf's "Big Bertha" range. Big Bertha started the ball rolling for oversized woods in 1991, with its larger and deeper club-head and a deep center of gravity. Callaway Golf's "Bigger Bertha" and "Great Big Bertha" woods remain ever popular, and offically acceptable after the USGA revised its initial proposal on the maximum size of club heads.

Materials

The "wood" is named after the material that the club heads were traditionally constructed of, with tough woods such as ash, beech, hazel, and persimmon most commonly used. Over the past three decades graphite shafts and titanium metal have replaced wood, as they are more durable and weigh less. At the turn of the century manufacturers introduced a new metal for shafts; scandium. Scandium is considered to be the material of the future for golf clubs, as scandium shafts are close to being perfectly symmetrical (unlike metal alloys). It is also proving popular for club heads. As scandium is a relatively new innovation it remains expensive, and titanium heads combined with graphite shafts remain the most popular option for woods as players gradually make the switch.

In your bag

Woods are numbered in terms of distance capability and the amount of loft offered by the angle of the club face, from 1-wood to 11-wood. The higher the number, the more accuracy and loft you get, while lower numbered clubs will make the ball travel further. A player should carry three woods, and most golfers opt for the 1-wood, 3-wood, and 5-wood. This combination allows you to tee off with a long drive, reach the green from the fairway, and get out of the rough.

WOODS AT A GLANCE

MAIN CHARACTERISTICS

- Designed for distance rather than accuracy

- Higher wood numbers mean higher accuracy

- Possess the longest shafts of all golf clubs

Advantage: Pack a punch
Disadvantage: Expensive

SIZE & DIMENSIONS

The size of the club head must not exceed 28.06 cubic inches (460 cm^3), although a manufacturing variance of 0.61 cubic inches (10 cm^3) is allowed.

The overall length of the club must be at least 18 inches (45.7 cm) and must not exceed 48 inches (121.9 cm).

BEST MATERIALS

Superior	Maraging steel
	Scandium
	Titanium
	Tungsten insert
Good	Stainless steel
Average	Aluminum
	Titanium alloys

Driver   *3-wood*   *5-wood*   *hybrid*

Clubs

1-wood ("driver"):

The only club specifically designed for teeing off, the 1-wood provides maximum driving distance and boasts the lowest lofts and longest shafts of all clubs. Traditionally, the loft was 9°–10° but technology means it is possible to purchase high-loft drivers up to 15°. The lower the loft, the lower the ball travels. Lofts vary, ranging from 7°–10° for professionals, 10°–12° for men, and 12°–15° for ladies. The most expensive individual club—which can cost up to $1,000—is nicknamed the "Big Dog" because it is the largest available club and has a massive sweet spot up to six square inches (52 sq cm).

2-wood to 5-wood ("fairway woods"): Used for teeing off, playing from the fairway, or out of the rough, these woods are easy to control, with their long shafts creating better swing speed and distance than irons. They have a smaller head than a 1-wood, with sufficient weight to deal with the rough. Most golfers favor the 3-wood and 5-wood, although the 7-wood and 9-wood are also useful.

6-wood to 11-wood ("hybrids"): Preferred by many over irons due to the "feel" they give when striking the ball.

Clubs: IRONS

Irons are thin, elongated clubs designed with either a cavity-back or a muscle-back to enable accuracy. These hollowed-out backs create a large sweet spot, with a thin face and hollowed area on the back differentiating a cavity-back club from a blade-style, muscle-back iron.

Materials

Despite the name, these clubs are not made of iron, but cast out of durable metals such as stainless steel or titanium.

In your bag

Like woods, irons are numbered in terms of their distance capability and the amount of loft offered by the angle of the club face. Irons range from 1-iron to 9-iron, and the higher the number, the greater the accuracy. Each higher numbered shaft is half an inch shorter. The lower the iron, the further the distance and steeper the loft, by 4°. Players should try to carry five irons, and many golfers select the mid-range 5-iron, 6-iron, 7-iron, 8-iron, and 9-iron so they have enough variety to provide a combination of control and distance for approach shots.

The grooves on the club faces of irons help to stimulate backspin, allowing the ball to stop close to where it lands. The performance of each specific club heavily relies on its grooves, so a swift clean with a tee and a towel is advisable after each shot. Generally, low irons are best for tee shots, mid-range irons for tackling the rough, and longer irons for chips and escaping bunkers.

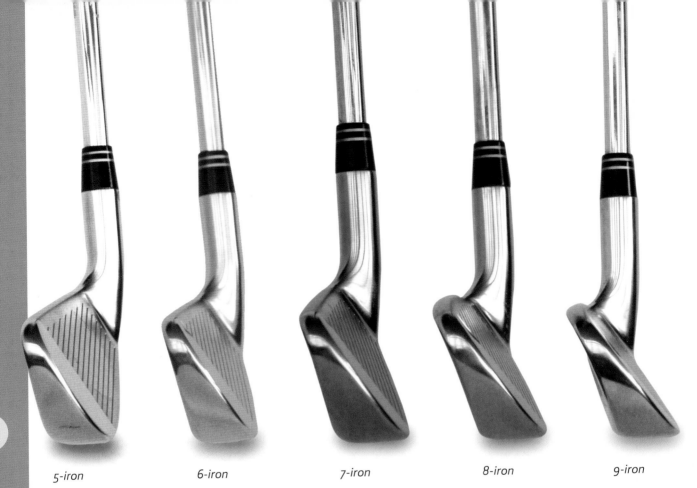

5-iron   *6-iron*   *7-iron*   *8-iron*   *9-iron*

Clubs

1-iron: Referred to as a "driving iron" as it can be used to tee off on short holes, although it is best left in the capable hands of experts.

2-iron: Only the foolhardy risk using this club as it is tricky to master. Experts fully utilize it to produce long, low, controlled shots.

3-iron: The longest iron found in a standard set of clubs. Worth a shot to tee off on long par 3 holes and long approach shots.

4-iron: Less intimidating than the 3-iron as it boasts a shorter shaft. Not widely used.

5-iron: Combines control with distance as it boasts sufficient loft to produce comfortable "feel." Useful for chip shots.

6-iron: Arguably the most popular club as it's the easiest iron to use, providing a happy medium of accuracy and distance.

7-iron: Used for short approach shots or to hit low when combating a strong wind.

8-iron: Guarantees consistent accuracy, backspin, and length, with a minimum roll.

9-iron: Used for delicate approach shots and chips around the green, or to pitch the ball long with a full swing.

Chipper: An iron with a loft greater than 10° designed for chip shots around the green instead of a 5-iron or 9-iron.

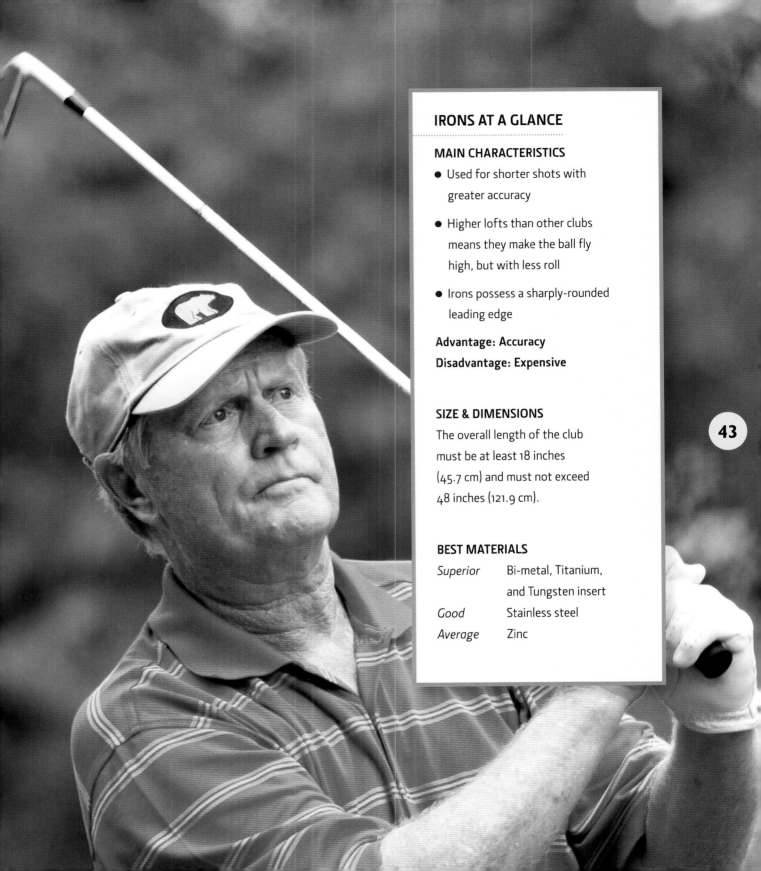

IRONS AT A GLANCE

MAIN CHARACTERISTICS

- Used for shorter shots with greater accuracy

- Higher lofts than other clubs means they make the ball fly high, but with less roll

- Irons possess a sharply-rounded leading edge

Advantage: Accuracy
Disadvantage: Expensive

SIZE & DIMENSIONS

The overall length of the club must be at least 18 inches (45.7 cm) and must not exceed 48 inches (121.9 cm).

BEST MATERIALS

Superior	Bi-metal, Titanium, and Tungsten insert
Good	Stainless steel
Average	Zinc

Clubs: WEDGES

Wedges are the club to opt for when faced with the challenge of getting over obstacles such as a greenside bunker or a water hazard, so a pitching wedge and a sand wedge play a vital role in your choice of clubs to carry. A pitching wedge follows on from the 9-iron in terms of loft and distance, while a sand wedge copes with deep rough around the green, as well as sand traps

Clubs

Approach Wedge
Also referred to as a "Gap Wedge" as it bridges the gap in distance between the pitching wedge and the sand wedge, with a loft of 52°. Used to great effect for approach shots.

Lob Wedge
With the highest loft—up to 60°—the ball travels the shortest distance of all wedges, but flies the highest. Used for delicate shots around the green and in the rough.

Pitching Wedge
Allows players to comfortably glide over hazards thanks to excellent "feel" and control achieved by a short, 35-inch (889 mm) shaft and a high loft on the club face of 48°–50°. Used for approach shots and chip shots.

Sand Wedges
Designed to escape bunkers, the high loft of 56°–58° allows the club to generate backspin as a result of heavy contact between the grooves of the club face and the ball. As well as sand

Lob wedge   *Pitching wedge*   *Sand wedge*

traps, it is used on the fairway and deep rough when a high shot with powerful backspin is necessary to overcome hazards prior to the green.

WEDGES AT A GLANCE

SIZE & DIMENSIONS

The overall length of the club must be at least 18 inches (45.7 cm) and must not exceed 48 inches (121.9 cm).

BEST MATERIALS

Superior	Bi-metal, Titanium, and Tungsten insert
Good	Stainless steel
Average	Aluminum, Titanium alloys

Clubs: PUTTERS

Putters are designed to be used on the short-trimmed grass of the green and play an influential role in deciding the outcome of individual holes. Putters are permitted to be adjustable for length and weight, and club makers are producing putters with longer shafts and two grips for increased control and feel. Chipper clubs—numbered 0 and 1—can be considered as "lofted putters" and can be used for short distances around the green

In your bag
The putter is arguably the most important club as it is used for just under half of the shots overall. Putters have a low loft, to reduce bouncing over the turf and increase the rolling distance, and are divided into rectangular-shaped "Blade Putters" and flat-soled "Mallet Putters."

Clubs
Blade Putters
Rectangular-shaped, which makes them easy to align for the putt. Very accurate, but lack a large sweet spot.

Mallet Putters
Designed with a round back and a large, flat sole resulting in a firmer connection with the ball.

Peripherally-weighted
The club's head is offset from the shaft to ensure excellent balance, which assists alignment.

Putter styles
Belly Putter
A belly putter has an extended shaft length of 41–46 inches (104–117 cm), designed to produce additional stability as the end of the shaft rests against the golfer's midriff.

Conventional Putter
Has a shaft length of 33–36 inches (84–91 cm). Designed for excellent control and feel, allowing the player to see the line between the ball and the hole. Golfers are required to lean forward in the stance

Long Putter
Also referred to as a "broomhandle" as an upright stance is required and golfers hit the ball with a "sweeping" action.

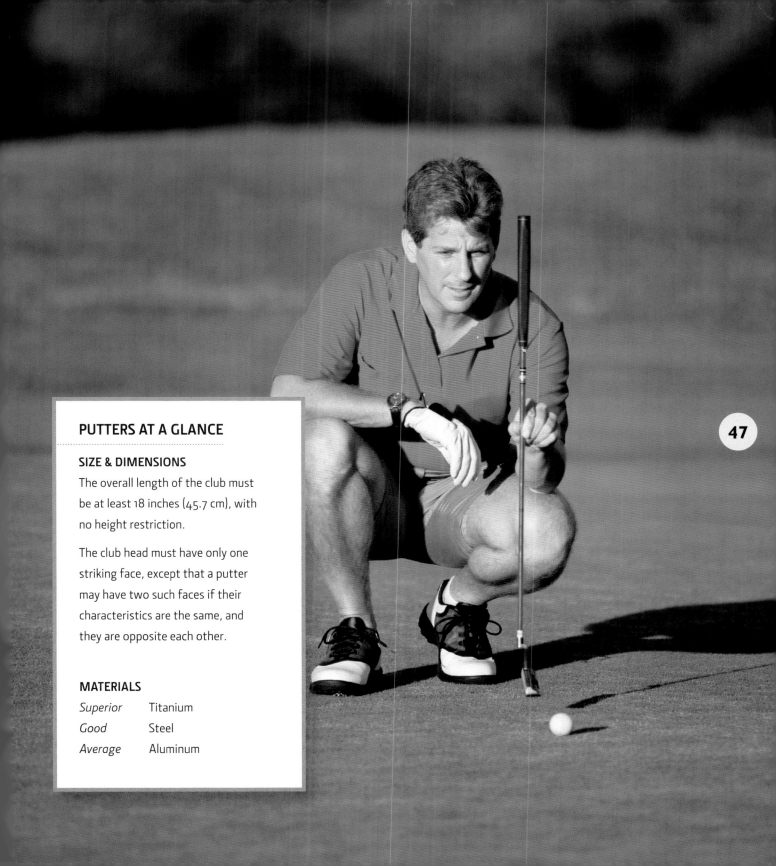

PUTTERS AT A GLANCE

SIZE & DIMENSIONS

The overall length of the club must be at least 18 inches (45.7 cm), with no height restriction.

The club head must have only one striking face, except that a putter may have two such faces if their characteristics are the same, and they are opposite each other.

MATERIALS

Superior	Titanium
Good	Steel
Average	Aluminum

As the "gentleman's game" is bursting with tradition, and the sport does not require a referee for friendly games, it is imperative to follow accepted behaviors and guidelines on a golf course. The onus is upon players to compete in the "spirit of the game," through a combination of honor, honesty, and sportsmanship.

The Rules of Golf are governed by the Royal & Ancient in St. Andrews, Scotland, and United States Golf Association (USGA). Since 1952, these two organizations have worked together to annually clarify, review, and revise the rules, and together they produce a rule book.

The rules themselves are complex and professional golfers are expected to know them intimately. For amateurs to appreciate and enjoy golf to its maximum potential it is worth becoming familiar with the rules, and this is especially useful for players who belong to golf clubs and compete in local tournaments. The rule book can also be consulted to clarify any disagreements or doubts between players. You can download the official rules from the R&A (*www.randa.org*) or the USGA (*www.usga.org*) websites for free, but for games between friends, the following guidelines show you what you can and can't do on the course.

Playing the game

BEFORE THE GAME

In its most common format (stroke play), the game of golf is scored in strokes. The aim is to achieve the lowest score by taking the fewest number of strokes over a round of 18 holes. The score can be noted as either the total number of strokes taken, or expressed in terms of "par" relative to the course par.

Each hole has its own par, which indicates the number of strokes that a professional golfer is expected to take to complete the hole. To determine the course par, the pars for all 18 individual holes are added together. If the course is par 72 and you hit 77, then you have a score of +5 (or "five over") whereas if your opponent finished the round in 70 their score would be -2 (or "two under"). Either way, the lowest scoring player is the winner.

Check the rules

Although the rules set by the R&A and USGA apply globally, it is important to check if any local rules have been imposed. These can be found on the back of each golf course's scorecard, so they will need looking at before you proceed to the first hole in case you need to make any enquiries before teeing off. You also need to make sure you have the right equipment in terms of balls and clubs, as covered on the following pages.

Balls

Before approaching the first tee, competing players should check with each other to see what brand of ball they are each using. Despite the availability of many different brands of golf balls, there is a tendency for golfers to play with the same few brands, and if a player is unable to identify their own ball during the game it is considered lost, which carries a penalty of one stroke. Ideally, players should add an identification mark to their golf ball—such as their initials—so it is clear whose ball it is.

At a glance...

Before the game

- Check the golf course's dress code in advance.

- Read the local rules on the scorecard and clarify anything you're unsure of before you head out.

- Check the golf course's boundaries on the scorecard.

- Mark your golf ball to identify it.

- Check you have the right number of clubs.

As well as ensuring you can identify your ball, you should also ensure that you have enough golf balls (and tees) before you start playing. You are not permitted to switch balls during a hole, but if a ball becomes damaged or lost during play you can change it, and you can also substitute a ball between holes.

However, some events—such as the PGA Tour—follow the so-called "One Ball Rule," which means you must play the same make and model of ball for the round. This rule will only apply if the tournament committee imposes it in competition conditions, or it is written into the local rules. For friendly games it isn't necessary.

Seasonal Rules

The majority of golf courses have seasonal rules, which during the winter months can include players being allowed to "play the ball up." This means that if you have a bare lie on the fairway (where the ball lies directly on hard ground without grass to raise it slightly) you are permitted to move your golf ball in order to improve your chances of hitting it cleanly.

GOLF CLUBS

Players are allowed to carry a maximum of 14 clubs during a game of golf, which includes woods, irons, wedges, and putters. Players who carry more than 14 clubs should be penalized by a single stroke for each additional club over the limited number. This penalty is applied to a player's overall score, not to each hole.

Despite being limited to 14 clubs, this still provides a sufficient array of clubs for you to play a round. Before you set off to the first hole you should always ensure the set of clubs in your bag includes a wood and driver to tee off, a range of irons for the fairway, wedges to tackle bunkers and the rough, and at least one putter. But make sure you have no more than 14 clubs in total.

If players opt to share a golf bag for their round (if they're playing as a team, for example), the number of clubs between them still must not exceed 14. But players who start the round with fewer than 14 clubs can add additional clubs during the game, but only if play is not delayed.

If you have any suspicion that an opponent has more than the permitted number of clubs in their bag you are allowed to check, but this really only applies during competitions or tournaments. If it transpires that more than 14 clubs are being carried by your opponent, then an official should be informed immediately.

Damaged clubs

It is imperative that clubs are chosen carefully because you can't switch out any of your clubs once you have started the game—even if one is damaged—although amateurs (but not professionals) are permitted to replace a club if it becomes completely unusable. Should a club become damaged during a game you can use it for the rest of the round, but only if you are not deliberately trying to break it in order to make it unfit for play. A player with a damaged club cannot borrow a club from another player, even if it is their only putter. However, as long as play is not delayed, a damaged club can be repaired or replaced by its owner.

52

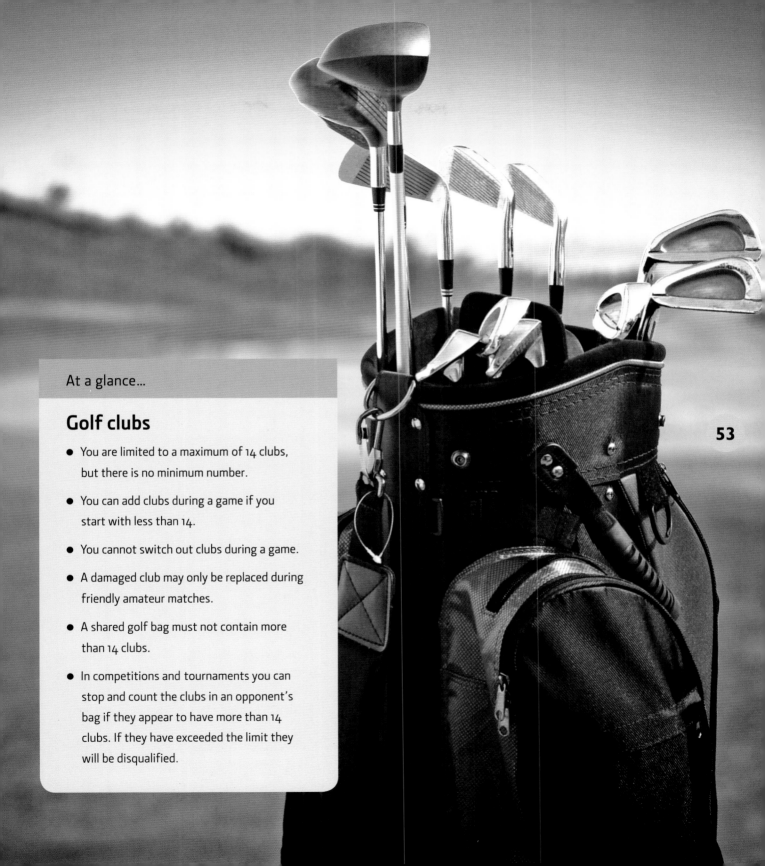

At a glance...

Golf clubs

- You are limited to a maximum of 14 clubs, but there is no minimum number.

- You can add clubs during a game if you start with less than 14.

- You cannot switch out clubs during a game.

- A damaged club may only be replaced during friendly amateur matches.

- A shared golf bag must not contain more than 14 clubs.

- In competitions and tournaments you can stop and count the clubs in an opponent's bag if they appear to have more than 14 clubs. If they have exceeded the limit they will be disqualified.

DURING A ROUND OF GOLF

As golf is a relatively quiet game, you should respect other players by staying as quiet as possible while they take their shots. Any sudden movement or sound could prove distracting, so treat your opponents—and team members—as you would like to be treated yourself.

During a game you are not allowed to ask for any advice from anyone except your caddie or playing partner, as this is deemed to give players an unfair advantage. In the same way, you shouldn't attempt to give advice to anyone except your playing partner.

You should also resist the temptation to play a practice stroke during a hole, although it is possible to take a practice stroke when the hole has been completed. This usually takes place on the green when a player has missed their putt, after all players have finished the hole.

Restricted areas

While you are out on the course, you need to pay close attention to any areas that are clearly marked as "restricted" or "under construction." If you miss-hit a shot, or it otherwise ends up in a restricted area or a part of the course that is under construction you are allowed to take a free drop ball. You can also take a free drop if your golf ball is just outside the area, but is deemed to be unplayable—for example, if it is against a rope or stake that marks the prohibited area.

54

At a glance...

During a round of golf

- Do not ask for advice from anyone except your caddie or playing partner.

- Do not give advice to anyone except your playing partner.

- You must not play a practice stroke while playing a hole—only after the hole.

- Be considerate towards other players on the course.

- Be aware of any restricted areas or parts of the course marked as under construction.

- Observe the local rules on golf carts.

Golf carts

If you opt to rent a golf cart—or bring your own to the course—then you need to observe the course's usage restrictions. Many golf courses will require you to strictly follow the "90 degree rule," which helps prevent fairway grass from becoming damaged. This means you are only permitted to take 90 degree turns when leaving the official cart path, to travel in a straight line to your golf ball. This stipulation (along with commonsense) means that you will avoid taking your golf cart across or on to important areas on the hole, such as teeing areas and greens. During wet weather or lengthy dry periods you will also find that the majority of courses will not permit you to drive your golf cart anywhere other than the cart path.

55

Little known facts about...

Advice during a game

- The 1858 rules originally stipulated that a player may not ask for advice, nor be knowingly advised, except by his playing partner.

- Giving unsolicited advice did not become a violation of the rules until 1947 (USGA) and 1952 (R&A) respectively.

ORDER OF PLAY

The golfer who takes the first shot in the teeing area on each hole has earned what is known as "the honor." This is based on the previous hole, with the player who finished with the lowest score teeing off for the next hole. If two golfers achieve the same score then the player that won the hole prior to the previous hole continues to have the honor.

To decide who has the honor on the very first tee, the golfer that hits first is usually determined by the toss of a coin, but when there is a group playing there is a tendency to mutually decide who plays first, before approaching the hole.

On the fairway, in the rough, or in a bunker, the golfer whose ball is furthest from the hole gets to strike first. This also applies to putting on the green, although if a ball is very close to the hole it is often conceded or putted down the hole so that it is not in the way of other players in the group. If a ball on the green is in the path of other golfers' balls there are two options; you can mark the ball then move it out of the way, or you can play it immediately to finish the hole, providing this is ok with your opponent(s).

Keep delays to a minimum

Once you have all played your shots on a hole you are expected to continue with minimal delay, to avoid holding up other players on the course.

Should your group find itself consistently playing slower than golfers behind you, you are expected to let them play ahead of you—effectively letting them pass you on the course. Likewise, if your group is playing faster than a

group of golfers ahead then you are likely to be signaled to play through. This tends to happen if two golfers are following behind a larger group, if the group in front has spent time searching for lost golf balls, or they are simply less experienced players taking longer on each hole.

Golf is a very time consuming sport and, within reason, players are expected to be ready to hit their shot when it is their turn. You may find that your patience as well as your skills are tested to the maximum if you get stuck behind a slow group, however you should aim not to hit your shot until the group ahead is safely out of your way. This particularly applies to the green and surrounding bunkers, as quite often you cannot see that far ahead due to the course layout.

Scoring

There are only two basic forms of play—Match Play and Stroke Play—which are covered in the following chapter. In both types of game, players are expected to keep their own score on individual scorecards, so it's up to you to enter the number of strokes taken to complete each hole.

This should be done at the end of every hole, but not while you're on the green, as it could cause delays to a group of golfers following you. However, you are expected to have recorded your score before teeing off on the next hole. By recording your scores at the end of each hole you will keep an accurate tally, and will be able to compare scorecards at the end of the game and determine the winner.

Little known facts about...

Scorecards

- Scorecards were not mentioned in the official rules until 1891.

- Only the marker's signature was necessary on scorecards from 1902 until 1947 (USGA) and 1950 (R&A) respectively.

- Scorecards now need to be signed by both the marker and the player. Failing to sign your own card can lead to disqualification.

57

HITTING THE BALL

The golden rule in golf is to play your ball as it lies on the course. There are a few exceptions to this— such as landing on ground under repair or if there is a man-made obstruction before the green—but generally, if your ball ends up in a tricky situation you must play it from that position. If your ball lies in a bunker or a water hazard, for example, you are not allowed to ground your club before your downswing, so in a bunker your club must not touch the ground before you strike the ball.

As well as not being permitted to improve the lie of your ball, you cannot unfairly alter the area around the ball if you feel it would interfere with your intended swing—or your line of play. So bending, breaking, or moving anything that is fixed or growing is not allowed.

58

Little known fact about...

Calling "fore"

If there is a danger that your ball could hit other players, you are obliged to shout "fore" as a warning alert. The origin of the cry first appeared in the official rules of 1875, which determined that a golfer and/or his caddie had to bellow "fore" prior to hitting the ball if there was even the remote possibility of others on the course being struck by a stray ball.

Teeing off

When it is your turn to tee off you must place your ball between the two colored markers you are using (male, female, senior, and so on) and up to two club lengths behind the front line of the markers. You should never tee off from in front of them, and certainly cannot move the markers, but as long as your ball remains within the set perimeter of the teeing area or tee box you are allowed to stand outside the teeing area to strike your ball.

In Match Play there is no penalty should you tee off from outside the marked area, although your opponent does have the option to request that you replay the shot. In Stroke Play the penalty is a little more severe, with two strokes applied for teeing off outside the marked area—making your next tee shot your third stroke for the hole, which must be taken from within the permitted area.

Missing the ball

Although it is unusual, players have been known to miss making contact with their ball, which is affectionately known as a "whiff." Intent is clearly the key during a game of golf, so each attempt to hit your ball counts as a stroke, even if you miss it completely. However, there is one exception to this, which applies to the ball on the tee: if the ball falls off the tee as you attempt to strike it, you can replace it without incurring a penalty stroke.

Little known fact about...

Golf ball inventions

In 1973, an innovative golf ball was fitted with a miniature transmitter inside it, which enabled the owner to track his ball via a radio receiver. The use of such a receiver and transmitter was frowned upon by the both the R&A and the USGA, with both authorities swiftly banning the ball from all official golf competitions.

59

THE BALL IN PLAY

In general, if you move your golf ball while playing a hole you will be punished by a penalty, although the nature of the penalty can vary. However, there are occasions when you can move it, such as when it ends up in an animal's hole, or any other abnormal ground condition, so here are a few of the reasons why you might need to move a ball, and the price you will pay for doing so.

Water hazards: If your ball ends up in a water hazard you can either re-take the shot from the same position (which counts as another stroke), take a drop ball penalty just behind the edge of the water that the ball crossed, or attempt to play the ball where it lies (if possible).

60

Little known fact about...

Out of bounds

The term "out of bounds" was originally found in the official rules of 1899 and carried a penalty of distance only. A ball was deemed to be out of bounds when more than half of it came to rest outside the golf course's recognized boundaries. Since 1950, the rules have stated that the entire ball must cross the marked boundary to be declared out of bounds.

Dirty ball

Many players are unclear whether you can clean a dirty golf ball, in case it counts as "interfering" with the ball, but this is not a complex issue. You are permitted to clean your ball between holes, but not midway through the hole. A single stroke penalty is imposed for cleaning a dirty ball while playing a hole, which means that you cannot rub any dirt off, even if you do not move the ball.

However, there are times when you can legitimately lift and clean the ball during a hole. The most common situation applies to being on the green, when you are permitted to lift a ball to prevent it obstructing another player, on the condition that you clearly mark its position. Failing to mark the ball on the green carries a one stroke penalty, but you are allowed to clean it once you have lifted it.

You can also lift, mark, and clean your golf ball if it finishes in a hole made by a burrowing animal, or in ground that's under repair. This is because players would need to confirm the ball's identity, so should your ball end up in a hole made by an animal you will not be penalized for lifting the ball and dropping it within one club's length of the creature's hole, but only on the condition that the dropped ball does not move any closer to the flagstick.

Dropping the ball

A number of situations in golf allow you to take a "dropped ball," and this should be done in a specific way, as follows:

You are expected to stand upright and hold the ball at shoulder height and arm's length before dropping it.

A dropped ball must be re-dropped if it strikes you, your playing partner, your caddie, or equipment, and if it rolls closer to the flagstick and hole.

Out of bounds: If you hit your shot and it ends up out of bounds the penalty suffered is one of both stroke and distance. Not only is a one stroke penalty applied, but you must drop the ball as close as possible to where it started from, and take the shot again.

Artificial obstacles: There is no penalty if your ball is blocked by an artificial obstruction on the course, which is essentially any man-made object that isn't part of the course—a golf cart, the green-keeper's mower, a rake, and so on. If you find yourself faced with an unplayable ball due to an artificial obstruction you can move either the ball or the obstruction (but not both).

Casual water: Casual water is water that isn't a water hazard on the course, such as a puddle. As it isn't part of the course you can take a drop ball, but no stroke penalty is applied. The ball must be dropped within a club's length of where the shot finished and must not be dropped closer to the hole on the green. The exception to this is if the puddle is in a bunker—you can't get out of the sand hazard just because there's water in it, so the ball should be dropped within the bunker.

GOLF BALL IN MOTION

The rules surrounding a golf ball in motion are pretty straightforward and simple to remember, and basically come down to who has deflected or stopped the ball. If you, your caddie, or your playing partner deflect or stop your ball while it is moving then you will receive a two stroke penalty (Stroke Play) or forfeit the hole (Match Play).

If your golf ball is deflected or stopped by an opponent, or someone unconnected to your game of golf, you have to play the ball as it lies and the same applies if your golf ball is deflected or stopped by another ball that's sitting on the course. There is no penalty, but you must play your ball as it lies.

There are exceptions to this, and in Match Play you can replay the shot—without penalty—if an opponent or an opponent's caddie inadvertently deflects the ball, while in Stroke Play you must replay your shot if another player or spectator accidentally deflects the ball onto the green.

Lifting the ball

On occasion, a ball may be temporarily lifted at the request of other players. This is most likely to happen if your ball is considered an obstruction that is preventing another player from taking a stroke. The golf ball should be marked before it is lifted, and replaced on this mark.

Ball at rest

If your ball is at rest (i.e. stationary on the course) and is moved by you, your playing partner, or your caddie, a one stroke penalty should be applied and you must return the ball to its original position. If someone else—or another golf ball—moves your resting ball, then it should also be put back to its original position, although this does not incur a penalty as it is not your fault.

Loose impediments

Although there is generally a penalty for moving a ball at rest, you can move any loose impediments that may be obstructing the ball, without penalty. Loose impediments are defined as objects such as leaves, stones, and twigs, but this term only applies to anything that is not growing or fixed in position. You can move any loose impediments, just as long as they are not stuck to your ball, and the ball or the impediments are not in a hazard. However, if you touch a loose impediment within one club's length of your golf ball and your ball moves, you will be penalized one stroke and your ball will have to be returned to its original position. This penalty does not apply to your ball when it is on the green.

Little known facts about...

Loose impediments

● The first reference to loose impediments was written into the original 13 rules of 1744 in Scotland. It applied to animal bones, break-clubs, and stones, which could only be removed if they lay within one club's length of the ball on the green.

● Players have always been allowed to remove loose impediments on the green, with loose soil and sand added to the list of impediments on the green in 1972.

63

UNPLAYABLE BALL

At any time, you can declare your ball as "unplayable." The player is the sole judge of whether the golf ball is deemed to have an unplayable lie, and your golf ball can be virtually anywhere on the course, except out of bounds or in a water hazard, for you to genuinely declare it as unplayable. However, it is vital that you play in the spirit of the game, so should only state that your ball is unplayable when that is the case.

If you declare a ball as unplayable you have several options. The first to consider is to take a dropped ball. If you decide to do this you can drop your ball within two club lengths of where it lies—but no closer to the hole—and take a one stroke penalty.

Alternatively, you can return to the original position and play the stroke again, taking both a one shot penalty and a distance penalty as your next stroke is likely to put your ball a similar distance from the hole.

Hazards and unplayable balls

You can declare your ball as unplayable when it is in a bunker, although that is a very rare situation. You can either drop the ball straight back into the bunker (to try and get a better lie), or replay the shot from its original position. However, you cannot declare a ball unplayable if it is in a water hazard.

A frequent problem that vexes players is when they hit their ball into a tree. Professionals—playing in competitions where every shot counts—are quite likely to climb the tree for the next shot rather than simply declare their shot unplayable, but most amateurs will probably take the easy option and forfeit a stroke with a dropped ball.

Unplayable ball:

- If you declare your ball as unplayable you can:

i) Play a dropped ball, taking a one stroke penalty.

ii) Take the shot again from the original position, taking a one stroke penalty.

- You can declare a ball as unplayable in a bunker, but not in a water hazard.

- If the ball lands in a puddle or similar casual water, or the burrow of a wild animal, there is no penalty for declaring it unplayable and taking a dropped ball.

65

LOST BALL

If you think you've lost your ball and have to start searching for it, you are restricted to a maximum time of five minutes to retrieve it to avoid delaying golfers following you around the course. In the spirit of the game, you should expect to be assisted by other golfers in your group, but if your search causes the group behind you to catch up with you, you should offer them the opportunity to play through rather than hold them up.

If you can't find and identify your ball within five minutes, then the ball is considered lost, and a one stroke penalty is applied. In addition, you must re-play the shot from as close as possible to the original position. However, if the ball was lost in either an abnormal ground condition or an obstruction then this doesn't apply, and a dropped ball is taken instead.

Of course, if you find your ball within the five minute period you can simply continue playing.

66

Little known fact about...

Provisional golf balls

The procedure for playing a provisional ball was introduced by St. Andrews in their rules of 1829. It was removed almost 30 years later as, at the time, this rule carried both a stroke and distance penalty.

The wrong ball

If you think you've found your golf ball it is not permissible to lift or touch the ball, except for identification purposes. However, you can declare the ball as unplayable and receive a stroke penalty to remove the ball from a hazard or unplayable lie.

If you decide to play the ball and it turns out that it is the wrong ball, then a two stroke penalty will be added to your score on the hole. In Stroke Play you would then have to return to play the correct ball or, in Match Play, forfeit the hole.

Provisional ball

Experience tells players if their miss-hit shot into the rough is likely to be recovered, and if you believe that you are likely to have lost your ball after hitting it you can choose to play a provisional second ball. You must clearly state to your group that you intend to use a provisional ball, otherwise it counts as striking the wrong ball, with a two stroke penalty applied as above.

Even if you declare you are playing a provisional ball, a penalty stroke should be added and the provisional ball should be replayed from the original position before searching for the original ball.

If your original golf ball is found while you are searching for it, then this must be played instead of the provisional ball—you cannot choose to continue playing the provisional ball instead, regardless of which ball has the better lie.

Little known facts about…

Lost golf balls

● Aberdeen golfers were responsible for introducing the five-minute time limit for lost golf balls in their rules of 1783.

● St. Andrews introduced the same time restriction in their rules of 1842, but removed it four years later. They subsequently introduced time limits of ten minutes (1882) and then five minutes again (1891).

● In 1899, when *The Rules of Golf* were formatted, the five minute rule was introduced, and to this day has not been altered.

WATER HAZARDS

It is vital that you familiarize yourself with the scorecard before starting to play, as it shows you the golf course's boundaries, and also determines what is considered a lateral or regular water hazard. Generally speaking, a lateral water hazard is one that runs along the side of the playing areas, while a regular water hazard will be on the course itself, such as a stream crossing the fairway, a pond, or even the sea on a traditional links course.

However, water hazards don't always have water in them. Water hazards have marked boundaries, and this may include a few feet of land surrounding the water itself. In summer months—as water levels drop, or a creek dries up—there may also be more land exposed, or a complete absence of water. The marked area still counts as a water hazard though.

Regular water hazards

If you think your ball is lost in a water hazard you may play a provisional ball from the same position, taking a one stroke penalty as described previously. You must inform other golfers in your group that you are about to hit a provisional ball, which will be abandoned if the original golf ball is subsequently retrieved.

At a glance...

Water hazards:

- If you think your ball is lost you can play a provisional ball from the original position, with a one stroke penalty.

- If your ball ends up inside the boundaries of a water hazard you can:

i) Play the ball as it lies.

ii) Play a dropped ball, taking a one stroke penalty.

iii) Take the shot again from the original position, taking a one stroke penalty.

- Striking the water while taking a shot in a water hazard results in a two stroke penalty (Stroke Play) or forfeiting the hole (Match Play).

If you choose not to play a provisional ball you should see where your original ball has landed. If you end up in a water hazard and are able to play the ball (if it's landed on the bank of a lake, for example) you can do so, but you must not touch the water prior to hitting your golf ball. This includes touching it with both the club face and your hand. If you do touch the water, a two stroke penalty applies in Stroke Play, while in Match Play you lose the hole.

If your ball has literally sunk without trace, you can play a dropped ball and take a one stroke penalty. The ball must be dropped behind the water hazard, in line with the hole and the point that it crossed the hazard's boundary. You may drop the ball any distance behind the hazard along this line.

Alternatively, you can return to the original position and take another shot, again with a one shot penalty.

Lateral water hazards

Should your ball come to rest in a lateral water hazard, the dropped ball scenario differs slightly. You can drop the ball up to two club lengths from the point it crossed the hazard boundary (the "inside" of the boundary), and you can also drop it on the opposite side of the hazard (the "outside") at an equal distance from the hole. In both cases a one stroke penalty applies.

Little known facts about...

Hazards

● Hazards have always been referred to in *The Rules of Golf*, and the first known set of rules from 1744 declared that: "Neither Trench, Ditch or Dyke, made for the preservation of the Links, nor the Scholar's Holes, or the Soldier's Lines, Shall be accounted a Hazard."

● However, hazards were not defined for almost two centuries. The first definition of hazards was written into the 1893 rules, and included an intriguing list that was deemed to hinder a fair lie of the ball. The definition of a hazard included "any bunker, water, sand, loose earth, mole hills, paths, roads or railways, whins, bushes, rushes, rabbit scrape, fences, ditches..." or anything that was not the ordinary green of the course.

69

OBSTRUCTIONS

You should check the golf course's scorecard to familiarize yourself with the local rules regarding both moveable and immovable obstructions as the rules can vary depending on where you play. In general, moveable obstructions (such as tin cans) can be moved without penalty from anywhere on the course, and if an immovable obstruction (something that is permanent, like a road) interferes with your stance or swing, you are permitted to drop your golf ball within one club's length, without incurring a penalty.

Objects

You can move natural objects that are not fixed or growing—such as a broken branch—without incurring a penalty, but a penalty is incurred if the obstruction is moved from either a bunker or water hazard.

Man-made objects such as the green-keeper's mower or rakes can always be moved without penalty, as they are not considered part of the course. If your ball lands in a bunker or water hazard then you can move man-made objects that are interfering with play, and if these are immovable you can take a dropped ball—again without penalty. The ball must finish no closer to the hole and flagstick, and should be dropped within one club length of its original position. However, as bunkers and water hazards are considered course hazards, you must drop the ball back into the hazard—you can't move it onto the fairway, or into an easier position outside the hazard.

Little known facts about...

Obstructions

● Obstructions were categorized together with hazards and loose impediments, but they have been gradually separated. What are now termed as obstructions and loose impediments were first defined as a hazard, which referred to virtually anything that prevented a golf ball's fair lie.

● In 1988, the rules were updated to include ice cubes and other forms of manufactured ice as an obstruction.

Bunkers

As a bunker is designed to be a challenge, you are not allowed to make contact with the ground of the bunker, either with your hand or with your club, prior to your downswing. Your club face can make contract with the sand and the ground during your shot, although you will still be penalized if you "push" or "spoon" the ball up rather than playing a fair shot. Following a shot out of a bunker, it is imperative that you rake away any of your footprints and markings that indicate that you have played out of the bunker.

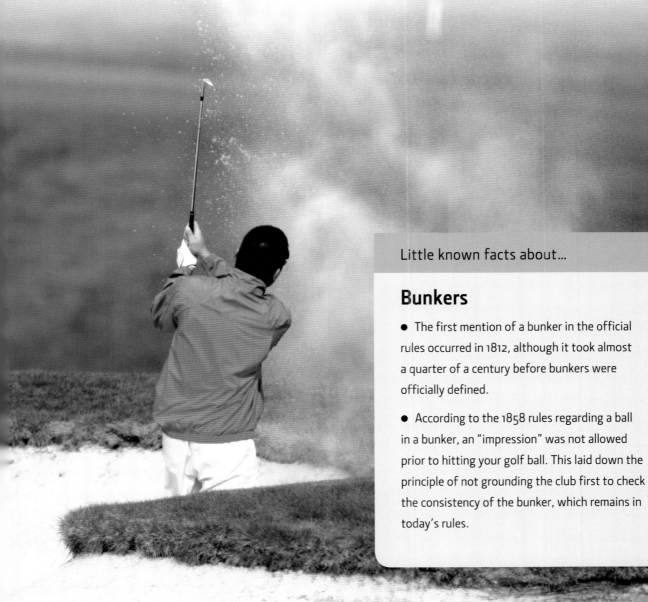

Little known facts about...

Bunkers

● The first mention of a bunker in the official rules occurred in 1812, although it took almost a quarter of a century before bunkers were officially defined.

● According to the 1858 rules regarding a ball in a bunker, an "impression" was not allowed prior to hitting your golf ball. This laid down the principle of not grounding the club first to check the consistency of the bunker, which remains in today's rules.

ON THE GREEN

Almost half of the overall strokes during a round of golf take place on the green, and its immaculately manicured surface is treated as if it is a religious place, with silence and respect toward other golfers. Therefore, it is important that you do not leave your bag of clubs on the green—just take a putter with you and leave the rest of your equipment on your golf cart or beyond the edge of the green.

In keeping with the general order of play, the golfer whose ball lies furthest from the hole has the honor of hitting first and players must wait for all golf balls to come to rest before taking their turn to putt. As putting is such a sensitive task, loose objects can be removed from the putting line, but a player cannot improve their line by pressing down on the ground or repairing any spike marks left by golf shoes.

However, there are certain tools that you can use on the green. A divot tool comes in useful for repairing any marks your golf ball caused when it landed, and you can also use it to repair any old hole plugs on your putting line. You are also allowed to use a marker to indicate where your ball is on the green if you need to lift it to allow another player to make their putt. You can also lift and clean your golf ball—but not switch it— prior to taking your putt.

The flagstick

When you and your group are all on the green, you can either have someone attend to the flagstick—ready to remove it as the ball nears the cup—or you can remove it at the start and lay it down. If you decide to remove it from the outset, avoid leaving it on the green.

The reason you need to attend the flagstick is because you will be severely penalized if your golf ball hits the flagstick while putting on the green; in Match Play you will forfeit the hole, while in Stroke Play you will incur a two stroke penalty. However, there is no penalty should your golf ball strike the flagstick if you are playing your shot from off the green.

Should your golf ball come to rest on the edge of the hole and be prevented from dropping by the flagstick, the ball is deemed to have been holed if it drops into the hole during the careful removal of the flagstick. It is advisable to have witnesses see you or your caddie remove the

flagstick to verify that the ball fell into the hole. However, it is not guaranteed that a ball in such a precarious position will end up in the hole after the flagstick has been removed.

Green practice

Scraping, or even rolling a golf ball over the green would count as testing the putting surface, so this is not allowed while the hole is being played, but may be done after your group has finished their shots on the green.

There is also a tendency for a player to practice the shot after being disappointed by a missed putt, but again, this is only permitted after your group has completed the hole, not during the

Little known facts about...

The green

● The modern-day green—known as the "hole green" and "table-land" during the 18th and 19th centuries respectively—did not become a distinct area on the course until 1875. Before that it wasn't prepared any differently to the rest of the golf course.

● The dimensions of today's holes on greens have remained the same since the sizes were written into the 1891 *Rules of Golf*.

● The flagstick was first referred to in the 1875 *Rules of Golf*, which stated that golfers could have the flagstick removed when they were approaching the hole.

hole. You should also avoid practice putts if it will delay a group that is playing behind you.

After your group has finished on the green you are expected to make sure you leave it in the same condition as you found it, and you must always leave the green before filling in your scorecards to avoid delays.

PLAYING THE GAME: SUMMARY

Teeing Off

- Tee off between the tee markers and up to two club lengths behind the line of the markers.
- Penalty for teeing off outside teeing ground:
  Replay shot (Match Play)
  Two stroke penalty and replay shot (Stroke Play)

Playing the ball

- The ball furthest from the hole is played first.
- Play the ball as it lies and do not improve it.
- Do not touch the ground in a bunker, or the ground or water in a water hazard before your downswing.
- Do not push or spoon the ball from a bunker.
- Penalty for playing a wrong ball (except in a hazard):
  Lose hole (Match Play)
  Two stroke penalty and replay shot (Stroke Play)

Ball lost or out of bounds

- Check the local rules on the scorecard to establish the course boundaries.
- You have five minutes to search for a ball, otherwise it is deemed lost.
- If you cannot correctly identify your ball it is considered lost.
- If your ball is lost outside a water hazard or out of bounds you must play another ball from the spot where the last shot was played. You will also incur a one stroke penalty in addition to the stroke you just played.

Provisional ball

- You can hit a provisional ball if you believe your ball may be lost. You must state it is a provisional ball before hitting it or you are considered to be playing the wrong ball.
- If the original ball is found, but not lost or out of bounds, you must continue with it and abandon the provisional ball.
- If the original ball is lost or out of bounds you must continue with the provisional ball and incur a one stroke penalty.

Unplayable ball

- If you believe your ball is unplayable you can drop the ball in place or replay your shot. Both options incur a one stroke penalty.
- A ball cannot be declared unplayable if it is within the boundaries of a water hazard.

Ball in motion is deflected or stopped

- Penalty if your ball is deflected or stopped by you, your partner, or your caddie:
  Lose hole *(Match Play)*
  Two stroke penalty and replay shot
  (Stroke Play)
- If a ball struck by you is deflected or stopped by someone else, play your ball as it lies without penalty, except:
  If an opponent or his caddie deflects the ball you have an option to replay the shot
  (Match Play)
  If the ball is deflected onto the putting green, you must replay it *(Stroke Play)*
- Ball struck by you is deflected or stopped by another ball at rest:
  Play the ball where it lies *(Match Play)*
  If both balls were on the green before you played a two stroke penalty is incurred *(Stroke Play)*

Ball interfering with play

- You may have any ball lifted if it could interfere with your play.

Ball at rest is moved

- If your ball is at rest and is moved by you, your partner, or your caddies—except as permitted by *The Rules of Golf*—or if it moves after you have taken up your stance, you incur a penalty stroke.
- If your ball is at rest and is moved by someone else, or another ball, you may return it to its original position, without penalty.

Loose impediments

- You may move a loose impediment unless it and your ball are in a hazard.
- If you have touched a loose impediment within one club length of your ball and your ball moves, the ball must be replaced. Unless your ball was on the green, a penalty stroke is incurred.

Obstructions

- Check the local rules on the scorecard for guidance on immovable obstructions.
- Moveable obstructions anywhere on the golf course may be moved, but if the ball moves as a result it must be returned to its original position.
- If an immovable obstruction interferes with your stance or swing, you may drop the ball without penalty, but not nearer to the hole.

Lifting, dropping, and placing the ball

- If a lifted ball is going to be replaced, its position must be marked.
- If a ball is to be dropped or placed in any other position, it is recommended that the ball's original position be marked.
- Stand upright and drop the ball from shoulder height and at arm's length.
- If a dropped ball accidentally hits you, your partner, your caddie, or your equipment it must be re-dropped.

Water hazards

- Check the local rules on the scorecard to establish what the club considers to be a water hazard and a lateral water hazard.
- If you enter a water hazard, play the ball as it lies or drop the ball with a one stroke penalty.
- Dropped ball in water hazards:

  Drop the ball behind the water hazard (on the opposite side to the hole), keeping a straight line between the hole, or play again from where you hit the ball into the hazard

- Dropped ball in lateral water hazards:

  Drop within two club lengths of the point where the ball crossed the boundary of the hazard, or at a point on the opposite side of the hazard that is equidistant from the hole

Casual water and ground under repair

- If your ball is in casual water, ground under repair, or a hole made by an animal, you may drop the ball without penalty.

On the green

- You can repair ball marks and old hole plugs on the line of your putt, but no other damage.
- You can mark, lift, and clean your ball but must replace it in the same position.
- Do not test the surface of the green by rolling a ball or scraping it.
- Penalty for hitting the flagstick when the ball is played from the green:

  Lose hole *(Match Play)*

  Two stroke penalty and replay shot *(Stroke Play)*

Winning the game

- The winner is the player who takes the lowest number of strokes for the round (Stroke Play) or wins the most holes (Match Play)

77

It is possible to play golf individually, in pairs, or in teams, but for each of these options there are only two playing formats—Match Play and Stroke Play.

The rules are similar for both, although there are some variations when it comes to scoring. Match play uses an obvious "player versus player" format, and the aim of the game is to score points by getting your ball in the hole first. The number of shots it takes to do this isn't necessarily important—it's the holes you win that counts most.

With stroke play you are competing more against the course, usually over a full round of 18-holes. Essentially, the aim is to use as few strokes as possible to match—or better—the par given to each hole. The final score is then determined by the number of shots each player/team has taken to play the entire round of golf, using the players' handicap ratings if applicable.

However, as we'll see in this chapter, within the match play and stroke play games there is a wide range of playing formats than can be played both socially and competitively.

Scoring

STROKE PLAY

Stroke play is the most common format of scoring, where the total number of shots taken is used to decide the winner. The player taking the fewest number of shots over a complete round of golf—or more holes if stipulated—is crowned the winner, with the lowest net score determining the winner if the competition includes the use of handicaps. This makes it the easiest form of scoring, and the one that is used for the majority of pro tournaments, including The Masters, The Open Championship, and the U.S. Open. Like the scoring, the penalty system used in Stroke Play is also simplistic, with a violation of *The Rules of Golf* leading to disqualification.

Golfers write down the number of shots that are taken on each individual hole, and these are recorded against the par score to make it simpler to compare scores between players. The time for writing down scores should be at the next tee, rather than delaying other players by comparing numbers on the green.

Referees aren't used to oversee stroke play games, so it's the players' responsibility to keep an eye on their opponent(s) to protect their rights and make claims when they think they have been wronged. Each golfer should have an interest in the scores and shots of other players, especially as a breach of the rules will result in being disqualified. Such violations of the rules can even include seemingly minor indiscretions—such as not assessing yourself a penalty stroke, or failing to sign your scorecard. Although disqualification seems a harsh penalty, it is part and parcel of the stroke play game.

Play-off rules

If there is a tie for first place at the end of a competition's stipulated number of holes, then there are a number of play-off rules implemented to determine an overall winner:

Aggregate play-off: A predetermined number or series of holes are played to decide the tie, although this could also result in a draw.

Eighteen-hole play-off: Like aggregate play-off, but a full round of 18 holes is played.

Sudden-death play-off: If an aggregate or 18-hole play-off fails to separate the players then "sudden death" can be used. As the name suggests, holes are played until one player scores lower than their opponent on an individual hole to win the game.

PAR FOR THE COURSE

Each hole is given a par number, which represents the number of shots with which a professional or scratch (zero handicap) golfer would be expected to complete the hole. Most holes range from par three to par five, although some par six holes exist. With two putts anticipated on each hole, the number of the par varies depending on how many shots are expected to be taken to safely position the ball on the green. For example, it should take one shot to the green on a par three hole, two shots to the green for a par four hole, and three shots to the green for a par five hole.

The total par of a golf course is the overall figure when the pars of all 18 holes have been added together.

Although scoring is based on the number of strokes taken, golf abounds with terms relating to how many shots a player has taken against par. If you've just walked into the clubhouse for the first time, this is what it all means:

Albatross	3 under par
Eagle	2 under par
Birdie	1 under par
Par	score matches the par for the hole
Bogey	1 over par
Double Bogey	2 over par
Triple Bogey	3 over par

MATCH PLAY

Match play is a game played by holes, with the fewest numbers of shots (or, for handicap matches, the lowest net score) winning the hole. The overall match can be won when the number of holes won is greater than the number of holes remaining to be played, so effectively the match is over when one team wins 10 holes.

THE RYDER CUP

The most famous event to use the match play format is the Ryder Cup, which gets international coverage as the United States take on Europe (including Great Britain) over a grueling series of 28 matches. Players use the foursome match format, alternating their shots, and a single point is awarded for each match that is won. The team that scores the most points from all 28 matches wins the Ryder Cup, and should the teams tie on 14 points, the current cup holders retain their title.

If there is a tie at the end of the 18 holes being played, the match is extended over an agreed number of holes until a winner is determined. The score is kept by noting the number of holes that are declared "all square" and "up" (see glossary at right), as well as those holes remaining to play.

Match play formats

Singles
The most straightforward match play format sees two players compete directly against one another, with the lowest score winning each hole.

Foursome
Foursome match play sees two teams—each consisting of two players—play against each other using an "alternate ball" format. Teams designate which golfer plays the tee shot from odd- and even-numbered holes, and for each hole the teams play only one ball. The players alternate shots until the hole is completed, and the team that achieves the lowest score wins. If the teams' scores tie, the hole is halved.

Fourball
Like foursome play, fourball is played by two teams of two players, but uses a "better ball" system, rather than the alternate ball. This means that each golfer plays their own ball, with four balls played per hole. Each of the four golfers achieves a score for the hole, with the lowest individual score winning the hole for the team. If opposing players both have the same lowest score, then the hole is halved.

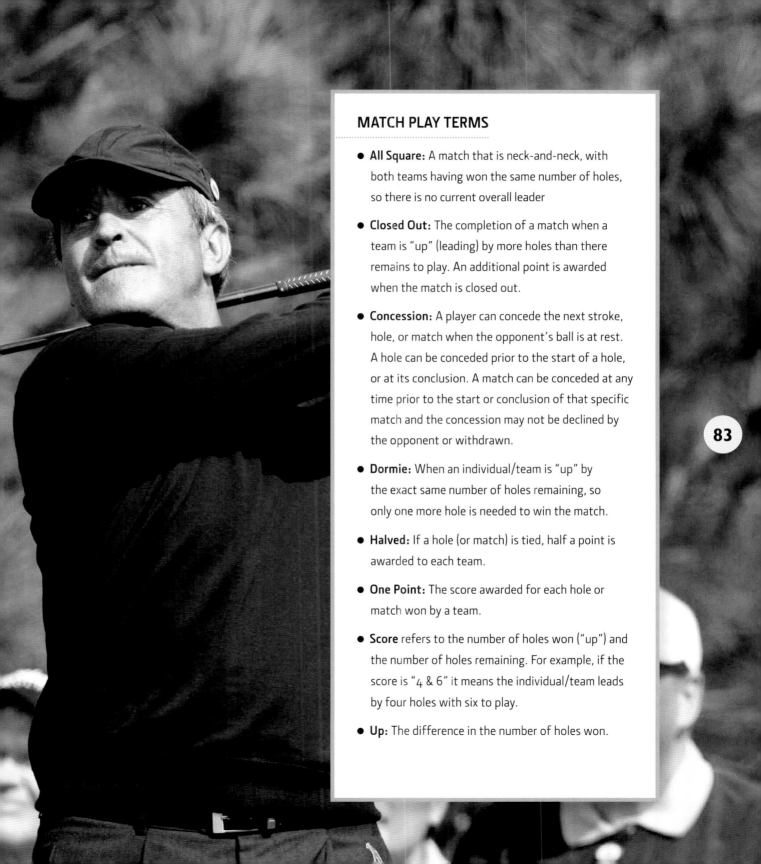

MATCH PLAY TERMS

- **All Square:** A match that is neck-and-neck, with both teams having won the same number of holes, so there is no current overall leader

- **Closed Out:** The completion of a match when a team is "up" (leading) by more holes than there remains to play. An additional point is awarded when the match is closed out.

- **Concession:** A player can concede the next stroke, hole, or match when the opponent's ball is at rest. A hole can be conceded prior to the start of a hole, or at its conclusion. A match can be conceded at any time prior to the start or conclusion of that specific match and the concession may not be declined by the opponent or withdrawn.

- **Dormie:** When an individual/team is "up" by the exact same number of holes remaining, so only one more hole is needed to win the match.

- **Halved:** If a hole (or match) is tied, half a point is awarded to each team.

- **One Point:** The score awarded for each hole or match won by a team.

- **Score** refers to the number of holes won ("up") and the number of holes remaining. For example, if the score is "4 & 6" it means the individual/team leads by four holes with six to play.

- **Up:** The difference in the number of holes won.

HOLE	M PAR		HCP	PLAYER
			1	
10	146	3	14	
11	63	3	5	
12	97	3		

EVERY PLAYER MUST HAVE A PUTTER

HANDICAP SYSTEM

The rationale behind a handicap system is for golfers to be on a level playing field, regardless of their ability and location. A handicap is a numerical representative of a golfer's playing potential, with the strongest players given the lowest handicaps. Once armed with a handicap, golfers can compete against each other all over the world, although only one handicap per player is permitted, even if a golfer belongs to two or more clubs.

In the United States, handicap-affiliated courses post a chart to indicate course handicaps for golfers, as the formula is complex and takes into account both the handicap index and the slope rating. A course handicap, expressed as a whole number, represents the number of shots required to reach the level of a "scratch" golfer. (Someone who plays off scratch has a handicap of zero).

Through the handicap system, golfers are permitted to deduct their course handicap from the round's gross score to calculate their net score. Both the PGA and the USGA use a number of different formulas to calculate handicaps, primarily consisting of Course Handicaps and Handicap Indexes.

Getting a handicap

Golfers must belong to an affiliated club to use the handicap system. A player's official handicap is called a handicap index, which a golfer achieves after posting the results from previous rounds. The actual number of rounds varies, depending on the official handicap authority, but once issued it determines the golfer's handicap index.

Once a player has a handicap index they can determine a course handicap—for almost any course they choose to play—using a chart supplied by the course or an online calculator at websites such as *www.myonlinegolfclub.com*. This tells them the actual number of shots they are allowed on a course, and is used to determine their final score. For example, if a golfer has a course handicap of 12, it means they can deduct 12 shots from their score over the full round of 18 holes. The maximum handicap varies for men and ladies (up to 28 or 36 respectively) and is not static—it constantly alters depending on recent results, so it can improve or deteriorate.

Formulas, formulas

A golfer's official USGA Handicap Index is a complicated formula, calculated using an adjusted gross score, course rating (indicated by the difficulty for scratch golfers), and slope rating (indicated by the difficulty for bogey golfers).

85

In the United Kingdom, handicap-affiliated golf courses are assessed for their difficulty and awarded a "standard scratch" so, for example, a par 72 course is rated as a standard scratch of 72. During competitions, the standard scratch is used to calculate handicap scores.

POPULAR COMPETITION FORMATS

Golf offers various scoring systems for playing competitions, which has led to numerous tournament formats being created. Many of these are suitable for social play, as well as for those who wish to take the game a bit more seriously.

Alternate Shot

Played by a pair of two-player teams, golfers in a team take alternate shots using the same ball. Also known as *Foursome*.

Best Ball

Played in teams of two, three, or even four. Each golfer in a team plays their own ball, with the lowest individual score in a team counted as the team score. The lowest team score wins the hole. Also known as *Fourball*.

Bingo-Bango-Bongo

Played by individuals, rather than teams, using a points system based on rewarding players for achievements on a hole, rather than the number

of shots. After the first stroke, shots are taken in the order of who is furthest away from the hole. Three points are awarded on every hole, with a single point given to the first player who:

- reaches the green first
- is closest to the hole once all the balls have reached the green
- putts their golf ball down the hole

The player with the highest overall score after the round is the winner.

Callaway

Played by individual golfers who do not have a verifiable (or very high) handicap, this format should even out the scoring in a consistent and fair manner. The golfers' net scores are what count, and these are calculated by a gross score that is deducted from the total number of shots played. A chart is used to allow individual players to deduct a set number of their worst holes, depending on their handicap, which gives every player the chance to win, even if they have had a couple of "nightmare" holes.

Chapman Pinehurst

Played by two teams, each with two players. A tee shot is individually taken by each golfer, with the balls switched between team members for the second shot (so Player A hits Player B's drive, and vice versa). From the third shot onward, the best ball of the two is chosen, and the golfers play alternate shots until the hole is completed.

Flags

Played by individuals, each golfer is given a specific number of strokes to play, depending upon their handicap. The player that either putts the ball down the hole, or gets the closest within their allotted number of strokes wins the hole.

Modified Stapleford

Played by individuals and teams. A stroke index is determined for each hole, with the number of shots allowed per hole dependent on the golfers' individual handicaps and the hole's stroke index. To calculate the score, the number of shots taken is deducted from (or added to) the expected number of shots. The highest score at the end of the match wins.

Peoria System

The Peoria System is a stroke-play handicap system suited to golfers without handicaps—or those with a high handicap—which can be used for tournaments. It's a fairly complex system, with golfers earning a "Peoria Handicap" at the end of their round, which is applied to their score.

The handicap is determined by six pre-selected holes, which are revealed by the tournament officials at the end of the round. A formula is used to work out the handicap by taking the total score over the six pre-selected holes, multiplying that number by three, deducting the par for the course, and reducing that figure by 80%. This gives the player a Peoria Handicap, which is deducted from their overall score for the round to give a net score. The net score can then be compared to the rest of the tournament players.

Example of how to determine a Peoria Handicap:

Golfer's total score for the round	98
Combined total over six pre-selected holes	32
Multiply the six hole total by three (3 x 32)	96
Par for the course	72
Deduct par for the course (96 – 72)	24
Reduce this to 80%	19
Player's Peoria Handicap	19
Apply handicap to total round score (98 – 19)	79
Golfers Net Score	**79**

Scramble

Scramble is played by teams of two, three, or four players and is one of the formats most often used for team tournaments. Golfers' individual handicaps are usually applied to their scores in two-player formats but not for four-player events.

After all the golfers tee off, the team's best shot is chosen, and all of the team's players take their second shot from this position. After the second shot, the best position is again chosen as the start of the third shot, and so on until the hole is completed.

Variations exist, such as *Ambrose Scramble* (where individual handicaps are used to calculate the final score), *Florida Scramble* (the golfer whose shot was selected as the best is not permitted to play the next shot), and *Texas Scramble* (where each golfer must play at least four tee shots over the round).

Stableford

Stableford can be played by individuals or teams, and can use either Alternating Shot, Best Ball, or Scramble formats. The scoring works on a points system, with points won or lost for each hole based on the following:

Double eagle	+8 points
Eagle	+5 points
Birdie	+2 points
Par	0 points
Bogey	-1 point
Double bogey (or worse)	-3 points

The Golf Record System

The Complete Golf Score Record System

Kona Country Club Golf Course, Hawaii

Mount Kidd Golf Course, Alberta, Canada

Harvest Golf Club, Kelowna, BC,

The game: Thursday, 13 March

Picture shows....

Add picture

Previous Record | Home | New Record | Delete Record | Print Record | List View | Quit | Next Record

Caption here....

Date	03/04/2008
Record No	0001
Course	Jericho National, New Hope, PA
Par	72
Rating	74.1
Start Time	8:30am
Tees Used	Black

Yardage 7,127
Slope 127
End Time 12:30pm

Add Picture   More Pictures

Conditions

Weather	Sunny
Wind	NW, Light
Temperatures	Low 80s

	Handicap	Gross	Net	Points
	12	90		

Players

		Handicap	Gross	Net	Points
Player 1	Me	5	87		
Player 2	Arnold Palmer	6	86		
Player 3	Jack Nicklaus	7	102		
Player 4	Tiger Woods				

Result in Match	Arnold won
Competition	Local
Match Format	Singles

Scorecard

	1	2	3	4	5	6	7	8	9	10	11	12	13	14	15	16	17	18	Totals
													5	4	4	4	4	4	
Par	3	5	4	4	5	4	3	4	5	3	4	5	4	4	7	6	4		
Score	3	6	5	8	10	9	4	8	9	4	3	2	1	2	4	2	2	1	
Putts	1	2	3	2	1	5	1	2	1	2	3	2	1						

Double Eagles/Albaross	0	(3 under par)
Eagles	3	(2 under par)
Birdies	2	(1 under par)
Pars/Evens	2	(Equal par)
Bogeys	2	(2 over par)
Double Bogeys	2	(2 over par)

Notes Notes here...

National, New Hope, PA

Picture shows......

Add picture

Add picture

Picture shows......

Add picture

Add picture

Whether you're just starting out, or have been playing golf for years, it's easy to see that a scorecard only tells a small part of the story of a game, match, or even a professional tournament. Golf is about more than the score you post at the end of a round; it's about the challenge of the course, time spent with friends, and the simple enjoyment of playing the game, regardless of whether you win or lose. Which is where *The Golf Record System* comes in.

The disc that accompanies this book contains a unique program that will not only let you record all of your scores from every round of golf you play, but it will let you add photographs, notes, comments, and much more about the day itself.

Whether you played with a friend, or as a group, *The Golf Record System* will help you preserve all your golfing memories, and this chapter explains how to use the program.

Using The Golf Record System

INSTALLING AND OPENING THE GOLF RECORD SYSTEM

Windows PC

Although you can run *The Golf Record System* directly from the CD, you won't be able to save any of your records or pictures, so you need to install the program onto your hard drive before you get started. Thanks to its intuitive, easy-to-use installer, you shouldn't have any problems installing *The Golf Record System*, and it will even add a shortcut to your *Start* menu to make it easy to find and open.

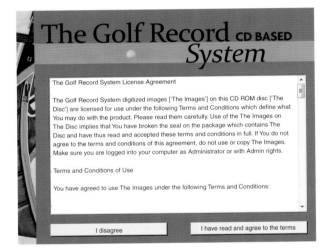

I have read and agree to the terms

1 Insert *The Golf Record System* CD. The disc license will automatically open—click *I Agree* once you have read the terms, then *Launch Installer Program* on the following screen.

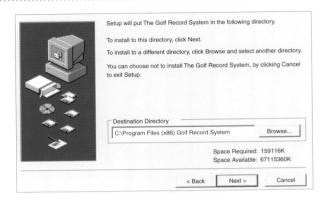

2 Follow the self-explanatory instructions on the *Welcome* screen, then click *Next* to go to the *Desination* screen. The default destination is your Programs folder, which is ideal. Click *Next* to continue, then *Next* at the *Confirmation* screen.

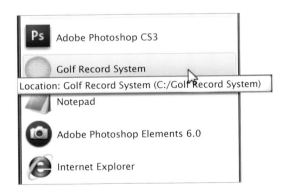

3 Windows will now install *The Golf Record System*, which will take a few moments. When the program is installed a shortcut to the program is automatically created in your Start menu. To start *The Golf Record System* just click on its name in your *Start* menu.

Apple Mac

Just like Windows PC users, if you've got a Mac you'll have no problem installing *The Golf Record System* onto your computer's hard drive using a simple drag-and-drop system. Once it's there you can add to your records whenever you like, to build up your collection of golfing memories.

① Start by inserting *The Golf Record System* CD into your computer's CD or DVD drive, and wait while it spins up. After a couple of second, the CD's icon will appear on your desktop. Double-click the icon to see the contents of the CD.

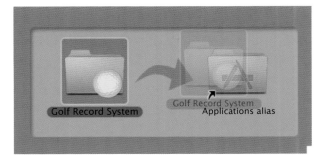

② To install the program, all you need to do is drag *The Golf Record System* folder onto the *Applications* alias in the installer window—your Mac will copy all of program files from the CD to your *Applications* folder. Once it's finished you can close the installer window and eject the CD.

Golf Record System

③ To open program, double-click on your computer's hard drive icon, and open the *Applications* folder. Locate *The Golf Record System* folder, double-click to open it, and then double-click *The Golf Record System* file to start the program.

Saving (Windows and Mac)

You will obviously want to make sure that all your golfing records are saved safely on your computer, so it might come as a bit of a shock that *The Golf Record System* doesn't have a "save" option.

Don't worry, this isn't an oversight—the program automatically saves every single thing you do. So when you add a score, it's immediately saved, and it's the same with pictures and any other text or notes you want to add—everything's safely stored the second you add it to your records.

93

CHOOSING YOUR BACKGROUND

When you open *The Golf Record System*, the first screen lets you choose the background image you want to be displayed behind your records. This background will apply to all your records, though you can change the background every time you open your records. You can also return to this *Home* screen at any time, so the background you choose is not fixed, allowing you to customize your records every time you open them.

The Golf Record System comes with 6 pre-installed backgrounds to choose from, covering some of the most famous courses in the world, including Augusta and The Old Course at St. Andrews, which you can see in greater depth later in the book.

To choose a background, click on the image that you want to use and you will be taken straight to your first record with that background in place. If you would prefer to have a plain background then click on the green, *Plain Background* button at the bottom right of the opening screen.

The Golf Record System

The Complete Golf Score Record System

Kona Country Club Golf Course, Hawaii

Mount Kidd Golf Course, Alberta, Canada

Harvest Golf Club, Kelowna, BC, Canada

13th hole, Augusta National

Palm Desert Resort, CA

Royal and Ancient, St.Andrews, Scotland

Click on a thumbnail image to select your score card background or click on the camera below to add your own

Add picture

Plain background

Adding a custom background

As well as using one of the pre-installed backgrounds you can also choose to use one of your own photographs instead. Any photograph can be used, whether it's a picture you've taken while you're playing, a shot of a favourite course or hole, or simply a family snapshot.

Add picture

① Start by clicking *Add Picture*— shown by the camera icon at the bottom left of the opening—or *Home*—screen.

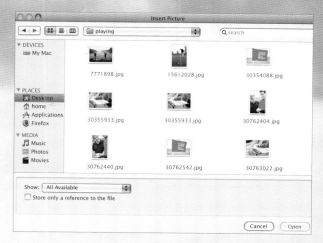

② Clicking *Add Picture* will open up a standard *Browser* window and you can look through your computer's hard drive—or external discs—for your favorite photograph. Maybe it's a picture of you making a stunning drive from the tee, or a tricky putt that got you a birdie to win a game you're proud of?

95

Background pictures

The Golf Record System is a rectangular, landscape shape, so the first thing you need to consider is the shape of the picture you want to use as a background. The program will automatically resize your photograph to fit the background, so it's probably not a good idea to use an upright (portrait format) photograph as this will be squashed to fit the landscape format of the records. Stick to longer, landscape-orientated photographs for the best result.

You also need to make sure that the photographs you use are saved in the right format. Most digital cameras take JPEG files (pronounced "Jay-peg") and this is the best format to use for the background because the files don't take up much space on your computer and are quick to load and display.

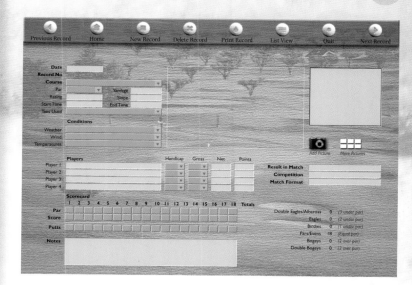

③ Once you've located the picture on your computer, click *Open* and you will be taken to your first record with your chosen background in place.

ENTERING AND EDITING RECORDS

The heart of *The Golf Record System* program is the *Main Record* view shown below. This is where you record all of the details from your round of golf you want to remember, such as where you played and who you played against, the weather, the wind, and even the time you started and finished your round. You can also enter your scores, view your vital statistics from a round,

and add pictures and comments to give more detail to the story of your round.

The following pages show you how to use this page to enter and edit information, and remember, because *The Golf Record System* automatically saves any changes everything can be edited, so nothing will be lost.

The *Main Record* view

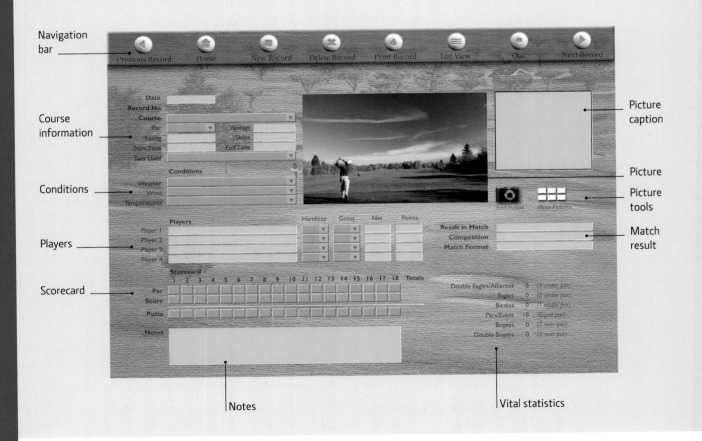

Date	03/04/2008		
Record No	0001		
Course	Jericho National, New Hope, PA		▼
Par	72 ▼	Yardage	7,127
Rating	74.1	Slope	127
Start Time	8:30am	End Time	12:30pm
Tees Used	Black		▼

Course Information

Date: Enter the date by clicking in the box and typing the date you played.

Record Number: This is generated automatically by *The Golf Record System.*

Course: Click on the drop-down arrow and choose your course from the list, or add one using the *Edit* option at the end of the list.

Par: Choose the course par from the drop-down menu or edit the list to add a different course par.

Yardage/Rating/Slope: You will find this information on your scorecard, or the course's website. Enter the information into the boxes.

Start/End Time: Type the time you started and finished your round

Tees Used: Choose the colored tees you used from the drop-down list.

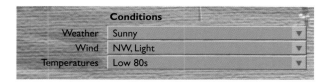

	Conditions	
Weather	Sunny	▼
Wind	NW, Light	▼
Temperatures	Low 80s	▼

Conditions

The weather and the wind can have an effect on your game; whether it's the sun in your eyes or a strong wind helping to carry your ball on certain holes. The **Weather**, **Wind**, and **Temperature** entries all use drop-down menus, which let you pick from a list, or use the *Edit* option to add your own specific entry.

Editing a drop-down menu

Many of the options use drop-down menus that let you choose from a number of pre-defined entries. It's easy to add a new entry though—just click *Edit* at the bottom of the drop-down menu and add what you want in the next dialog window. The next time you use that menu, your new entry will be there as well.

97

Navigation bar

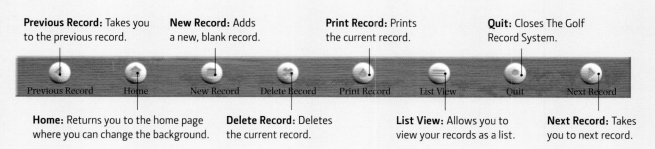

Previous Record: Takes you to the previous record.

New Record: Adds a new, blank record.

Print Record: Prints the current record.

Quit: Closes The Golf Record System.

Previous Record   Home   New Record   Delete Record   Print Record   List View   Quit   Next Record

Home: Returns you to the home page where you can change the background.

Delete Record: Deletes the current record.

List View: Allows you to view your records as a list.

Next Record: Takes you to next record.

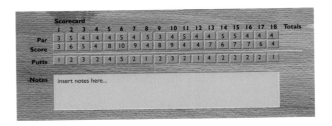

	Players	Handicap	Gross	Net	Points
Player 1	Me	12 ▼	90 ▼		
Player 2	Arnold Palmer	5 ▼	87 ▼		
Player 3	Jack Nicklaus	6 ▼	86 ▼		
Player 4	Tiger Woods	7 ▼	102 ▼		

Scorecard

	1	2	3	4	5	6	7	8	9	10	11	12	13	14	15	16	17	18	Totals
Par	3	5	4	4	4	5	4	5	3	4	5	4	4	5	5	4	4		
Score	3	6	5	4	8	10	9	4	8	9	4	7	6	7	7	6	4		
Putts	1	2	3	2	4	5	2	1	2	3	2	1	4	2	2	2	1		

Notes: insert notes here...

Players

You can type in the names of the people you played against in the boxes, with up to four names allowed (including your own).

For each player you can also enter a **Handicap** and **Gross Score**, using editable drop-down menus. Using the handicap and gross score you can then calculate your—and your oppenents'—**Net Score**, which is worked out by deducting the handicap from the gross score. You can simply enter the net score into the **Net** box.

If you are playing a match play game, rather than stroke play, you can use the **Points** box to record how many holes each player won, rather than the overall number of strokes.

Scorecard

When you enter the **Par** for each hole on the course, and the number of strokes you took (**Score**), the scorecard will show you how well you played each round. You can break your game down further by entering the number of **Putts** you took on each hole. Just click on a box and a drop-down list will appear for you to choose from. Over time this will let you see whether it's your driving game that's letting you down, or you need to hone your skills on the green. You can even add **Notes** to remind yourself what went wrong on a particular hole, or which clubs worked particularly well in certain situations.

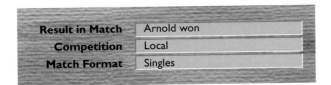

Result in Match	Arnold won
Competition	Local
Match Format	Singles

Match Result

This part of your record lets you summarize the round. In the **Result in Match** box you can either enter the winner's name, or—if you want to make this a more personal record—you can enter your standing after the round. You can also enter the **Competition** you were playing (if it was a competitive match) and the **Match Format** you played, whether it was stroke play, match play, or maybe a round of Bingo-bango-bongo.

Vital statistics

As you enter your scores for a round, *The Golf Record System* will work out how well you've played each hole against par in terms of Eagles, Birdies, and so on.

Double Eagles/Albaross	0	(3 under par)
Eagles	2	(2 under par)
Birdies	3	(1 under par)
Pars/Evens	7	(Equal par)
Bogeys	4	(2 over par)
Double Bogeys	2	(2 over par)

Pictures

Although your scorecard will give you a pretty accurate record of your round of golf, it isn't the same as a picture, which can show the weather conditions and give a literal snapshot of the game. You can add a picture for each and every record you create, and it can be anything from a photograph of you teeing off taken by a friend, to your group celebrating a hard fought contest at the 19th hole.

Add picture

1 To add a picture, click on the *Add Picture* camera icon to the right of the picture window.

2 Find the picture you want to use in the *Browser* window that opens, and click *Open*.

Adding a caption

Your picture will appear in the picture window for the record. If you want to add a caption to describe what the photograph's about, click in the green text box to the right of the picture window and enter it.

Adding more pictures

You can add more pictures to a record using *The Golf Record System's Gallery* feature. To access the gallery, just click on *More Pictures* to the right of the picture window.

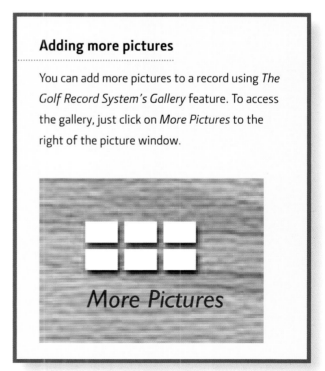

THE GALLERY

A single photograph will only tell one small part of the story of your day, so the *Gallery* section of *The Golf Record System* is a fantastic way of adding more pictures of your round—and it doesn't just have to be pictures of you or your friends playing. It could be the moment the skies opened and you found yourself sheltering from a torrential downpour, or the sun rising at the start of a pre-dawn tee time, or setting at the end of a long day. Of course, it could just as easily be a friend struggling to get out of the bunker, or a personal "hero moment" as you tee off on the final hole—essentially you can add any pictures that give you a flavor of the round you played and the enjoyment you had.

Image formats

The Golf Record System will run quicker if the photographs you use in the gallery are JPEG files. Unless you're a photographer (in which case you'll probably already be familiar with different file types), it's fairly safe to assume your digital camera will already be recording JPEG files. You can check this by looking at any of the photographs on your hard drive—if they have .JPG after them, they are JPEG files.

If they aren't, you will need to open them in an image-editing program such as Adobe Photoshop Elements, and re-save them.

100

Adding pictures to the gallery

1 Click *More Pictures* from the *Main Record* view to open the gallery window. You will see there is space for six photographs, and the first one is your current record picture.

2 To add some more pictures click the *Add Picture* camera icon next to an empty picture window on the *Gallery* screen.

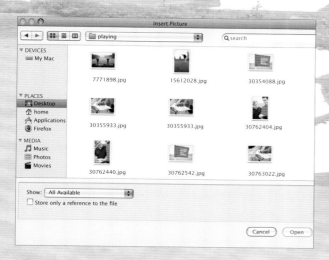

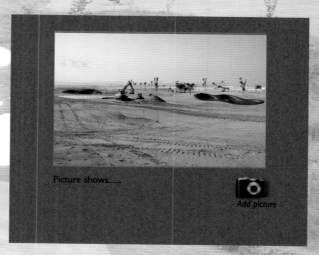

3 Use the *Browser* to find your next photograph and click *Open* to add it to your gallery.

4 Continue adding photographs using the *Add Picture* button next to the empty picture windows.

Adding captions

While they say a "picture speaks a thousand words," sometimes you can forget exactly what those words were, but adding a caption to each of your photographs will ensure you remember why you took the picture to start with and why it's important. To add a caption, click in the text box beneath the photograph. You can then enter your caption.

Once you've finished adding pictures and captions click *Back to Record* at top of screen to go back to the record view.

Replacing pictures

You can update the gallery for any particular round at any time you like, even if you have already added six pictures. For example, if your friend emails you a great photo from a round you played together, you can drop it into the gallery, replacing one of your existing pictures.

To do this, click *Add Picture* next to a picture box and choose the new photo from the *Browser*. The original picture will be replaced by the new one, but don't forget to change the caption as well!

THE LIST VIEW

The *List* view is the part of *The Golf Record System* that will let you see how your game is improving, and, in a single screen, let you view all of the rounds you've played. Essentially, it's an overview of every record you've entered, showing the date you played, the course you played on, and your score, broken down to show each individual hole, as well as your total for the round and the course par. In the list view, every game you play is available to you "at a glance" and you can order it in a number of ways to compare and contrast your fortunes on the course.

			Home		New Record		Delete Record			Print Record			Full Record			Quit							

Game	Date	Course	Hole: 1	2	3	4	5	6	7	8	9	10	11	12	13	14	15	16	17	18	Total	Par
0001	01/05/08	Jericho National, New Hope, PA	3	6	5	4	8	10	9	4	8	9	4	4	7	6	7	7	6	4	111	72
0002	01/12/08	Lookaway GC, New Hope, PA	6	5	4	7	5	4	6	3	6	4	7	5	7	4	4	4	5	4	90	75
0003	01/30/08	Mountain View, Trenton, NJ	6	5	6	4	4	5	4	5	5	6	3	5	4	6	4	3	5	4	84	70
0004	02/05/08	Rivercrest GC, Doylestown, PA\	5	6	5	6	4	4	6	10	5	5	4	6	6	5	7	5	4	6	99	72
0005	03/05/08	Makefield Highlands GC, Yardley, PA	5	5	5	5	4	6	6	7	5	3	5	3	3	4	5	5	4	5	84	70
0006	03/12/08	Makefield Highlands GC, Yardley, PA	5	6	5	4	4	5	6	6	6	5	4	7	5	5	4	6	4	4	91	72
0007	03/13/08	Makefield Highlands GC, Yardley, PA	4	5	5	5	4	5	6	4	4	6	5	8	3	4	4	5	4	6	86	74
0008	03/26/08	Jericho National, New Hope, PA	4	5	4	4	5	6	5	5	6	7	6	7	6	5	6	8	6		101	72
0009	03/28/08	Hopewell Valley, Pennington, NJ	6	5	5	4	5	4	4	3	4	5	5	4	5	5	6	5	4	6	85	72
0010	04/05/08	Jericho National, New Hope, PA	4	5	5	4	6	5	4	4	6	6	5	4	5	3	5	5	5	4	85	70
0011	04/07/08	Jericho National, New Hope, PA	4	4	4	5	2	5	6	7	5	4	5	3	5	5	4	6	5	4	93	72
0012	04/24/08	Jericho National, New Hope, PA	7	4	4	5	4	4	5	5	3	5	6	5	6	4	5	4	6	4	86	72
0013	04/28/08	Mountain View, Trenton, NJ	4	5	7	8	7	8	7	6	8	7	9	7	5	6	5	6	5	6	116	68
0014	05/21/08	Hopewell Valley, Pennington, NJ	3	6	5	4	8	10	9	4	8	9	4	4	7	6	7	7	6	4	111	72
0015	07/21/08	Rivercrest GC, Doylestown, PA	6	5	4	7	5	4	6	3	6	4	7	5	7	4	4	4	5	4	90	75
0016	07/22/08	Royal Lytham St Anne's, UK	6	5	6	4	4	5	4	5	5	6	3	5	4	6	4	3	5	4	84	70
0017	08/06/08	Stonybrook GC, Hopewell, NJ	5	6	5	6	4	4	6	10	5	5	4	6	6	5	7	5	4	6	99	72
0018	10/12/08	Jericho National, New Hope, PA	5	5	5	5	4	6	6	7	5	3	5	3	3	4	5	5	4	5	84	70
0019	10/24/08	Jericho National, New Hope, PA	5	6	5	4	4	5	6	6	6	5	4	7	5	5	4	6	4	4	91	72
0020	10/29/08	Jericho National, New Hope, PA	4	5	5	5	5	4	5	6	4	4	6	5	8	3	4	4	5	4	86	74
0021	12/01/08	Hopewell Valley, Pennington, NJ	4	5	4	4	5	6	5	5	6	6	7	6	7	6	5	6	8	6	101	72
0022	12/10/08	Jericho National, New Hope, PA	6	5	5	4	5	4	4	3	4	5	5	4	5	5	6	5	4	6	85	72
0024	12/25/08	Jericho National, New Hope, PA	4	5	5	4	6	5	4	4	6	6	5	4	5	3	5	5	5	4	85	70
0025	01/05/09	Jericho National, New Hope, PA	4	4	4	5	2	5	6	7	5	4	5	3	5	5	4	6	5	4	93	72
0026	01/09/09	Jericho National, New Hope, PA	7	4	4	5	4	4	5	5	3	5	6	5	6	4	5	4	6	4	86	72
0027	01/15/09	Jericho National, New Hope, PA	4	5	7	8	7	8	7	6	8	7	9	7	5	6	5	6	5	6	116	68
0028	02/16/09	Jericho National, New Hope, PA	3	6	5	4	8	10	9	4	8	9	4	4	7	6	7	7	6	4	111	72
0029	02/27/09	Jericho National, New Hope, PA	6	5	4	7	5	4	6	3	6	4	7	5	7	4	4	4	5	4	90	75

Navigation Bar

Home: The Home button takes you back to the opening screen of *The Golf Record System*, so you can change your background, or add a new one.

Delete Record: If you want to delete a record then just press Delete Record. You'll be asked if you're sure before the record is removed for good.

Full Record: To see more details about a particular round, click on the game number and press Full Record to be taken to the *Main Record* view.

| Home | New Record | Delete Record | Print Record | Full Record | Quit |

New Record: New Record creates a fresh record in *The Golf Record System* and returns you to the main record window covered on pages 96-99.

Print Record: If you want to print your list, then Print Record is the button to press. You'll be taken to the print dialog window, as described on pages 104-107.

Quit: Hit Quit to close *The Golf Record System*. Any changes you've made will have been automatically saved, so don't worry.

Game	Date	Course	Hole:	1	2	3	4	5	6	7	8	9	10	11	12	13	14	15	16	17	18	Total	Par
0001	01/05/08	Jericho National, New Hope, PA		3	6	5	4	8	10	9	4	8	9	4	4	7	6	7	7	6	4	111	72
0002	01/12/08	Lookaway GC, New Hope, PA		6	5	4	7	5	4	6	3	6	4	7	5	7	4	4	4	5	4	90	75
0003	01/30/08	Mountain View, Trenton, NJ		6	5	6	4	4	5	4	5	5	6	3	5	4	6	4	3	5	4	84	70
0004	02/05/08	Rivercrest GC, Doylestown, PA\		5	6	5	6	4	4	6	10	5	5	4	6	6	5	7	5	4	6	99	72
0005	03/05/08	Makefield Highlands GC, Yardley, PA		5	5	5	5	4	6	6	7	5	3	5	3	3	4	5	5	4	5	84	70
0006	03/12/08	Makefield Highlands GC, Yardley, PA		5	6	5	4	4	5	6	6	6	5	4	7	5	5	4	6	4	4	91	72

Sorting records

Every new record that you add is given its own **Game** or **Record Number**, and the default method for the list view to display your rounds is in numerical game/record order, starting at 001. However, this is just the order you entered the records, and not necessarily the order you played your games—if you find an old scorecard you thought had been lost you may want to enter the details of a game you played years ago. If that's the case, then you can also view the list in date order, simply by clicking the **Date** tab at the top of the list. In fact, you can order the list pretty much as you want—just click at the top of each column to display your records by **Game**, **Date**, **Course**, or even your **Total Score**. If you choose **Course** or **Total Score**, then your records will be put into alphabetical or numerical order, with the records then ordered chronologically.

In this way you have the freedom to view the information the way you want to—whether you want to see how you've progressed at a single course over a period of time, or just want to take a look at your all time best scores. You can also print out the list once you've re-ordered it, so you've got a reference.

PRINTING AND SHARING YOUR RECORDS

Although *The Golf Record System* will record all of your golfing endeavors on your computer, you will undoubtedly want to share your achievements on the course with friends, family, and maybe even the other players at your club. The easiest way to do this is to print them out, but you might also want to email them, or maybe even add them to a personal website. The following pages will walk you through printing—whether it's a full set of records, an individual round, or a list view summary—as well as giving a few hints and tips about the other things you can do to share your memories.

Printing a full set of records

Assuming you're just starting to enter your old scorecards into *The Golf Record System*, and adding your pictures and note, the first prints you'll want to make will most likely be of a full set of records. This isn't a difficult exercise at all, although you do need to make sure you set your paper and print sizes properly so each record page fits neatly onto a single sheet of paper.

1 Start by opening a record in the main view window and click the *Print Record* button.

2 By default, the *Page Setup* is set to Letter sized paper. It is also scaled to 75% and set to landscape orientation so each record will fit neatly on a single sheet of paper.

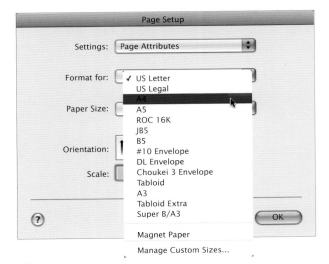

3 If you need to change the paper size (perhaps to A4), use the drop-down *Paper Size* menu. Click *OK* when you're done.

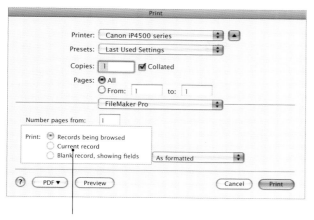

1. Make sure *Records being browsed* is checked or highlighted next to the *Print:* options

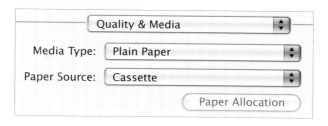

4 You will now be shown the *Print* dialog window, which will vary depending on your printer and operating system, so don't be surprised if yours look a little bit different to this one. However, the key settings are the same for every printer and the three most important things to do are:

2. Check you have the correct type of paper set, such as plain paper or photo paper.

Print Mode:
- ○ Printing a top-quality photo
- ○ Printing tables and charts
- ◉ Printing a composite document
- ○ Detailed Setting

□ Grayscaled Printing

3. Choose if you want to print in color or black and white.

105

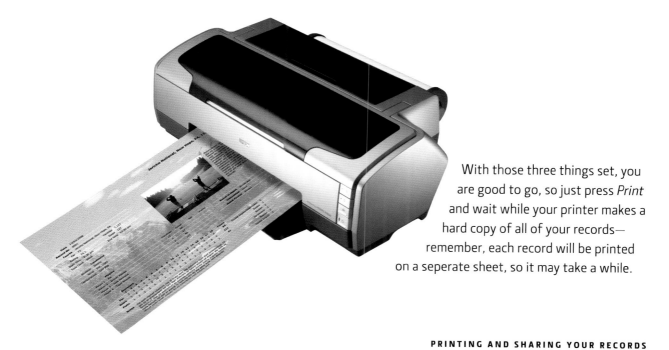

With those three things set, you are good to go, so just press *Print* and wait while your printer makes a hard copy of all of your records— remember, each record will be printed on a seperate sheet, so it may take a while.

Printing a single record

Printing a full set of records is great if you've just started adding to *The Golf Record System*, but if you've already got a few of your records printed out, you might not want to use your ink and paper printing duplicates. In this case, you can print out individual records if you want to, and it also gives you the chance to change the background image if you want to. If you want to change the background, simply go to the *Home* screen and choose the background you want for your printed record. Then, with your background set, navigate to the record you want to print and click *Print Record* as before.

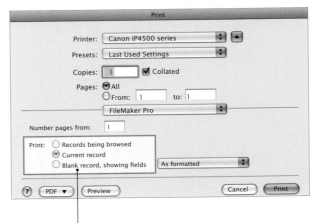

① Printing a single record doesn't differ too much to printing a full set, so go through Step 2 as described on the previous page to check the paper size is correct. When you have made sure everything is set correctly, click *OK*.

② As before, you'll be taken to the *Print* dialog window, and you can set your printer to the correct type of paper and choose whether you want your record printed in black and white or color. However, this time round, choose *Current record* from the *Print:* options, and not *Records being browsed*. This tells *The Golf Record System* just to print the record you are looking at, and not all of them. Click *Print* and your single record will be printed for you.

Printing the list view

Printing from the list view is essentially the same as printing all of your records from the main record view—you need to click *Print Record*, then check and set your *Page Setup*. When the *Print* dialog appears, choose *Records being browsed* from the *Print:* options to print out all of the records in your current list. This may need several pages, depending on how long your list is.

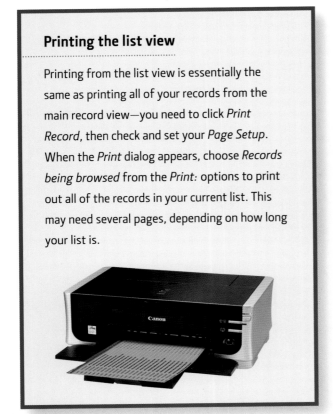

Exporting a record (Windows)

As well as being able to print your records using your desktop printer, you can export them as a digital file that is perfect for emailing to your friends to share your records.

1 To start, click on the *Print Record* icon to open the print window.

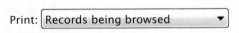

2 From the drop-down *Print:* options, choose whether you would like to save *Records being browsed* (all records), the *Current record*, or a *Blank record* (perhaps to take with you to a round of golf, to fill in while you play?)

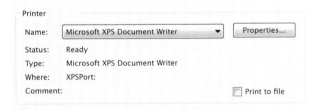

3 To create a file, rather than print a page, choose *Microsoft XPS Document Writer* from the *Printer Name:* options. Click *OK*, and choose a name and a location to save the file to.

4 The saved XPS file can now be opened using *Microsoft XPS Viewer*. This program is pre-installed in Windows Vista and available as a free download from the Microsoft website (*www.microsoft.com*) for Windows XP users.

Exporting a record (Mac)

Exporting a record using a Mac follows a very similar process to a Windows PC, although Macs will save PDF (Portable Document Format) files. A PDF can be read by a wide range of programs, including *Adobe Acrobat Reader* which can be downloaded for free from Adobe's website (*www.adobe.com*). PDF files are also compatible with both Mac and Windows computers, so it doesn't matter which system the person you are sharing it with is using.

1. To export a PDF, click *Print Record* to open the print window and choose *Adobe PDF* as your printer.

2. Select *Filemaker Pro* from the third drop-down menu, and decide whether you want to print all records (*Records being browsed*), the *Current record*, or a *Blank record*.

3. When you click *Print* you will be asked to name the file and choose somewhere to save it. Once saved you can attach it to an email to share your success on the course with your friends.

107

With so many pristine, world-class golf courses around the globe you can experience phenomenal challenges, whether playing golf is part of a vacation or the reason for a vacation. In every region on the planet there is one course that stands head-and-shoulders above the rest; one course that can claim to be that territory's golfing Mecca.

Whether it has some great historical standing, or it's the destination for the world's top players as they compete in a prestigious tournament, the four courses that follow are the ultimate from the four corners of the globe. These are courses that provide the perfect combination of a daunting challenge, with the added thrill of following in the footsteps of legendary players. To play passionately in the spirit of the game on any of these treacherous courses is the ultimate in golf, so even if your shots are mercilessly punished, expect an unforgettable experience in prestigious surroundings as you walk on hallowed turf.

Top courses

AUGUSTA NATIONAL GOLF CLUB (U.S.A.)

Augusta National Golf Club, 2604 Washington Rd, Augusta, Georgia 30904-5992
www.augusta.com

The fantastically scenic Augusta National Golf Club was designed by top golf course architect Dr. Alister MacKenzie, under the instruction of legendary player Robert Trent Jones, Jr. Opened in 1933 on the site of a former nursery, the course is still resplendent with fabulous flora, and the 635-acre course bears more than a passing resemblance to a typical British links course, which was part of Jones Jr.'s brief. Rolling hills lead onto alluring large greens with few bunkers, with fast putting areas containing subtle breaks.

One of the most exclusive private courses in the world (which lists Bill Gates among its most famous members), Augusta does not offer online tee times to the general public, and women have yet to be accepted into the club, but this is hardly surprising for the course that plays host to the annual U.S. Masters competition. As arguably the world's most prestigious golf event, fans flock to the course every spring to see how the greatest players on earth will cope.

Yet for all the high-rollers on the 300+ member list, and the draw of the Masters, MacKenzie would probably not be impressed with many of the modern, sharp-edged bunkers, as they are certainly not integrated into the natural surroundings like his original vision. And he would be outraged by the 12th and 15th greens, which have been heavily revamped since his innovative designs.

Augusta National Golf Club (as used for The U.S. Masters, 2008)

Hole	1	2	3	4	5	6	7	8	9	10	11	12	13	14	15	16	17	18	Total
Par	4	5	4	3	4	3	4	5	4	4	4	3	5	4	5	3	4	4	72
Yards	455	575	350	240	455	180	450	570	460	495	505	155	510	440	530	170	440	465	7,445
Meters	416	526	320	219	416	165	411	521	421	453	462	142	466	402	485	155	402	425	6,808

Hole 1

TEA OLIVE

Distance: 455 yards / 416 meters

Par 4

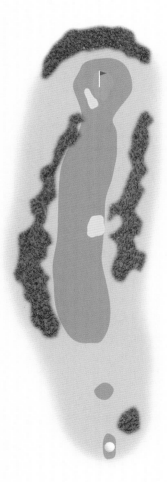

Hole 2

PINK DOGWOOD

Distance: 575 yards / 526 meters

Par 5

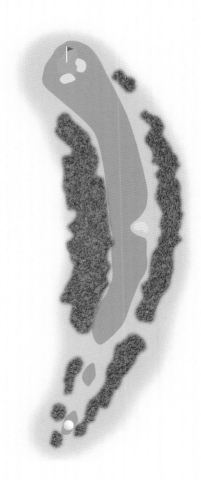

Jack Nicklaus, a six-time Masters champion, believes that the opening shot of the day is the most important. Yet the nerve-wrenching drive off the first tee has been extended by 20 yards (18 m) since 2005, to bring the fairway hill into the equation—with a bunker you definitely don't want to find.

The longest hole on the course was lengthened in recent years and suits big hitters. The slight dogleg is hazardous for prudent players and those who do not possess long drives, while the fairway bunker is a tricky trap. Two large, deep bunkers protect the entrance to a green that slopes from the back to the front.

Hole 3
FLOWERING PEACH
Distance: 350 yards / 320 meters

Par 4

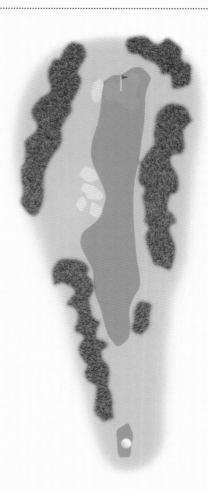

Arguably one of the best par 4s in the world, which is perhaps confirmed by the fact that it has not been altered in almost three decades. Trickier than it appears, it entices big hitters to get as close as possible to the small, pear-shaped green.

Hole 4
FLOWERING CRAB APPLE
Distance: 240 yards / 219 meters

Par 3

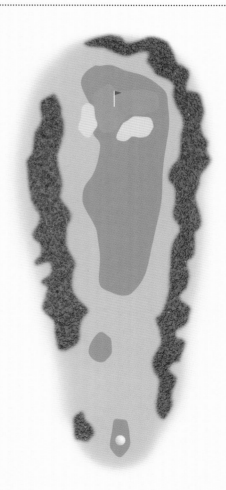

The elusive flagstick on this short hole can be reached with either a wood or low-iron in one shot, depending on the swirling wind conditions. The tricky tiered green is guarded by two deep bunkers, but once on the sloping green it is a great opportunity to grab a birdie.

Hole 5
MAGNOLIA

Distance:	455 yards / 416 meters

Par 4

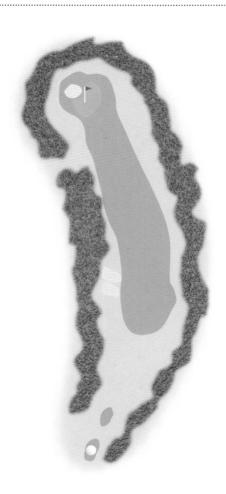

Hole 6
JUNIPER

Distance:	180 yards / 165 meters

Par 3

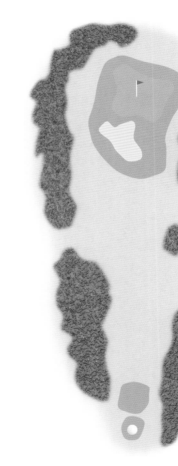

Inspired by the Road hole at St. Andrews, Magnolia has been lengthened by 20 yards (18 m) in recent years, making it a long par 4, and made even harder by the increased amount of rough. The dangerous fairway bunkers have also been enlarged, exaggerating the dogleg.

Getting close to the flagstick on this short uphill hole is more of a challenge that it appears. In the 1930s, the elevated green was fronted by a stream, and two decades later by a pond. The hazard was removed in 1959, and the hole has not been altered further since 1975.

Hole 7
PAMPAS

Distance:	450 yards / 411 meters
Par 4	

Hole 8
YELLOW JASMINE

Distance:	570 yards / 521 meters
Par 5	

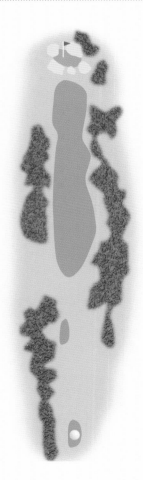

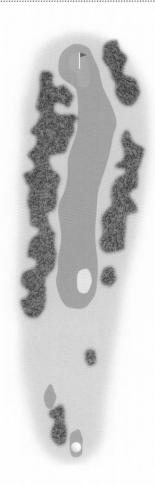

Arguably the tightest hole on the course, recent alterations have seen the tee extended, tree adjustments along the fairway, and a reshaped green that's protected by three lethal bunkers in front and two behind.

Despite the vast length, Yellow Jasmine could be one of the easiest holes on the course. Big hitters will relish playing this lengthy hole, as it is reachable in two strokes, but it needs an accurate tee shot to avoid the reshaped fairway bunker on the right side.

Hole 9
CAROLINA CHERRY
Distance: 460 yards / 421 meters

Par 4

Hole 10
CAMELLIA
Distance: 495 yards / 453 meters

Par 4

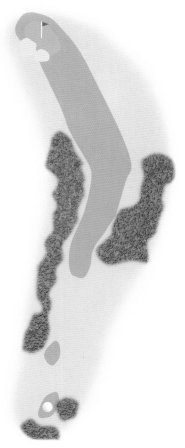

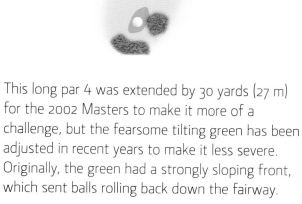

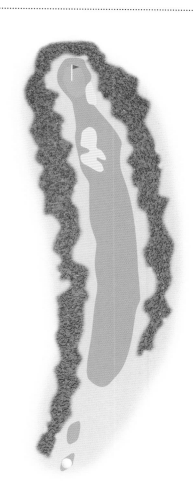

This long par 4 was extended by 30 yards (27 m) for the 2002 Masters to make it more of a challenge, but the fearsome tilting green has been adjusted in recent years to make it less severe. Originally, the green had a strongly sloping front, which sent balls rolling back down the fairway.

A dramatic long hole that plays sharply downhill and ranks as the most difficult hole at the Masters overall. The green—which tilts right to left—is tricky to reach, with a bunker sitting at the front, while the punishing slope will penalize shots hit too far left, short, or slightly long.

Hole 11:
WHITE DOGWOOD

Distance: 505 yards / 462 meters
....
Par 4
....

Hole 12
GOLDEN BELL

Distance: 155 yards / 142 meters
....
Par 3
....

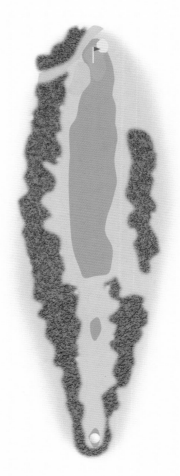

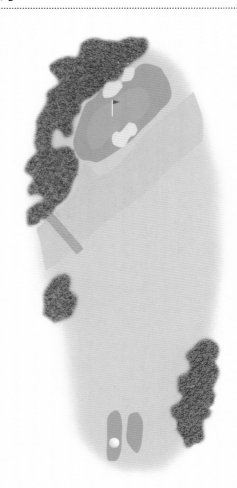

The start of the "Amen Corner," three holes (11-13) so-named after a 1958 article in *Sports Illustrated* claimed that if a par was achieved, golfers would whisper "amen." This very difficult water hole has been made more challenging in recent years through a lengthened tee, the introduction of pine trees, and a severely narrowed fairway.

Arguably golf's most famous par 3. Despite being the shortest hole on the course, it is treacherous because of the swirling wind and the narrow green, which is protected by water at the front and two bunkers behind, although three players have hit a hole-in-one here during the Masters.

Hole 13
AZALEA

Distance: 510 yards / 466 meters

Par 5

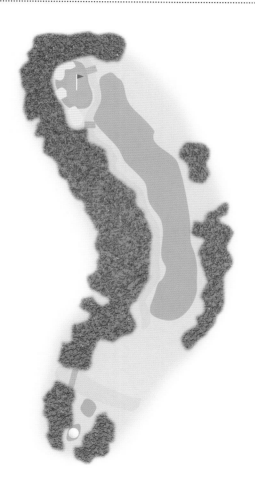

Hole 14
CHINESE FIR

Distance: 440 yards / 402 meters

Par 4

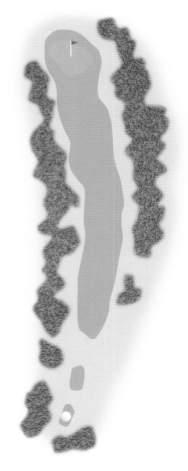

With around 1,600 azaleas stretching from the tee to the green, many golfers are distracted from the dangers that lie in wait. Rae's Creek flows down the left of the fairway and runs in front of the tiny green, which also has four small bunkers lurking behind it.

The only Augusta hole without a bunker, Chinese Fir makes up for it with a green that is considered to be one of the most challenging in golf. Three putts are fairly common due to a putting area that sharply slopes from left to right, making it virtually impossible for the ball not to roll away from the flagstick.

Hole 15
FIRETHORN

Distance: 530 yards / 485 meters

Par 5

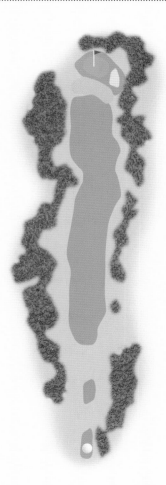

Hole 16
REDBUD

Distance: 170 yards / 155 meters

Par 3

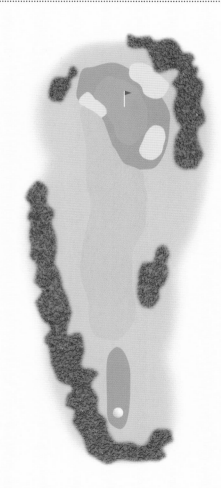

In 1935 the Masters was put on the world map courtesy of Gene Sarazen's famous albatross, after his stunning 235-yard (215 m), 4-wood approach shot became known as "the shot heard round the world." This is unlikely to be emulated as the tee area has since been extended by 30 yards (27 m).

Dr. Alister MacKenzie's hole is similar to the 12th (Golden Bell), with the water hazard introduced in 1947. This entire hole has no fairway, instead it is played over water toward the dramatically tilting green. Two bunkers will trap any misjudged tee shots on the right, while a small bunker guards the left.

Hole 5
HOLE O'CROSS (out)

Distance: 568 yards / 519 meters

Par 5

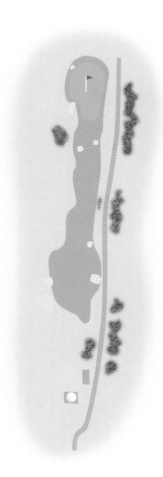

Arguably the easiest hole on the course, a birdie opportunity is on the cards for both excellent putters and big hitters. Once on the hard, acre-and-a-half green (which it shares with the 13th hole) you could find yourself faced with an enormous putt.

Hole 6
HEATHERY (out)

Distance: 412 yards / 377 meters

Par 4

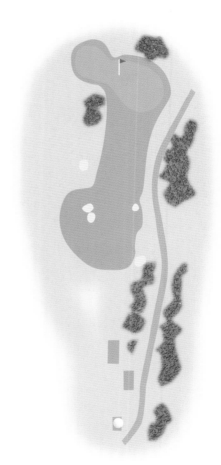

A further opportunity to hit a birdie on the front nine, especially as the fairly flat green is not guarded by bunkers. Just be sure to avoid the aptly named "Coffin" bunkers on the way, which can have a death-like effect on your scorecard.

123

Hole 7
HIGH (out)

Distance:	390 yards / 357 meters
Par 4	

Hole 8
SHORT (out)

Distance:	175 yards / 160 meters
Par 3	

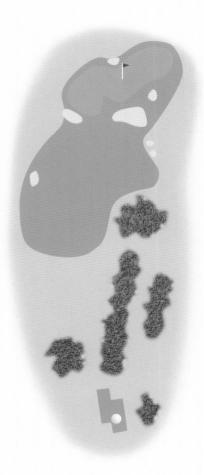

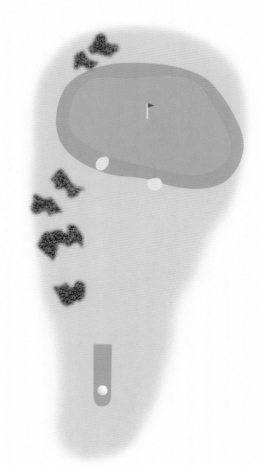

Another excellent opportunity for a birdie if you can steer the ball clear of the bunkers. A solid tee shot should clear any dangers, leaving a simple short pitch on to the heavily sloping green. Beware though, as the hollows and humps make the putting area unpredictable.

This short hole deserves respect for numerous reasons. The sole par 3 on the front nine, the vast green is played blind from the sheltered tee and is obscured by a notorious bunker that guards its entrance.

Hole 9
END (out)
Distance: 352 yards / 322 meters

Par 4

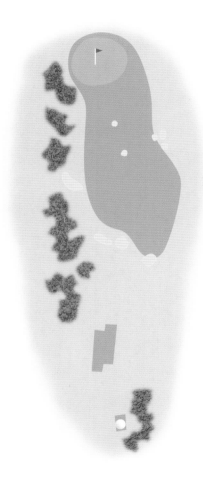

Hole 10
BOBBY JONES
Distance: 380 yards / 347 meters

Par 4

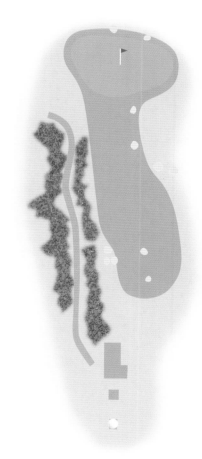

With its large fairway and a flat, circular green, End poses few problems; even the pair of deep pot bunkers that sit in the center of the fairway can be avoided quite easily with a little careful planning. The name refers to the fact that this is the turning point of the course—the "end" of the front nine holes.

Named in honor of the iconic golfer who died in 1971, power players were driving to the green with such regularity that the tee area was extended in 1998. Big hitters still relish the challenge of carrying their ball over the fairway and onto the flat, yet tricky, green, which doubles up with the 8th hole.

Hole 11
HIGH (In)

Distance: 174 yards / 159 meters

Par 3

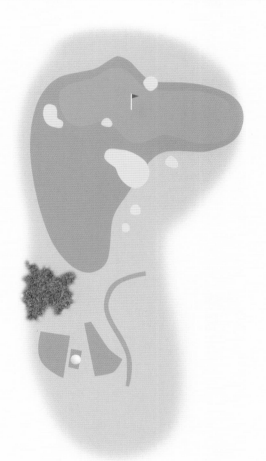

Hole 12
HEATHERY (in)

Distance: 348 yards / 318 meters

Par 4

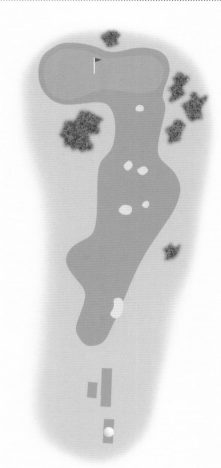

Running in the opposite direction to the exceptionally short 8th hole, this is the only other par 3 on the course. The tiny, yet deep, Strath bunker on the front edge of the sloping green obscures the flagstick.

Another superb birdie opportunity, despite the danger of five obscured bunkers down the center of the fairway, and gorse bushes on either side. The target is difficult to reach, protected by a steep slope and a bunker at its entrance.

126

Hole 13
HOLE O'CROSS (in)

Distance: 465 yards / 425 meters

Par 4

Hole 14
LONG HOLE

Distance: 618 yards / 565 meters

Par 5

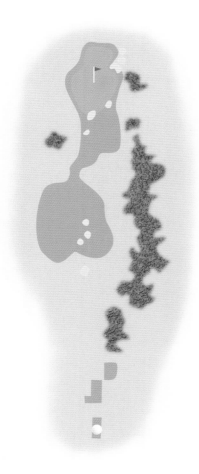

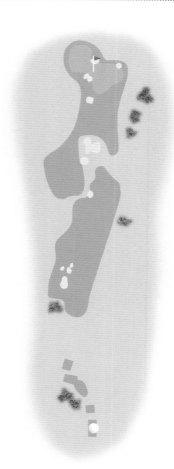

One of the course's toughest holes, made even more difficult in recent years since a new tee added 35 yards (32 m). The deadly Coffin bunkers lie 290 yards (265 m) from the tee, and will penalize inaccurate big hitters.

A treacherous par five that proved costly for Jack Nicklaus at the 1995 Open when he scored 10 for the hole, which included three shots trying to escape Hell bunker. Since then, the hole has been extended to 618 yards (565 m) to become the longest hole in Open history.

Hole 15
CARTGATE (in)

Distance: 456 yards / 417 meters

Par 4

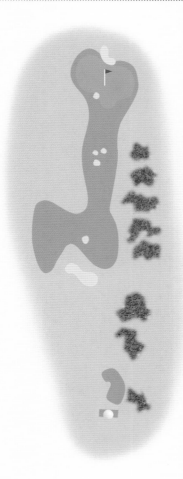

Hole 16
CORNER OF THE DYKE

Distance: 423 yards / 388 meters

Par 4

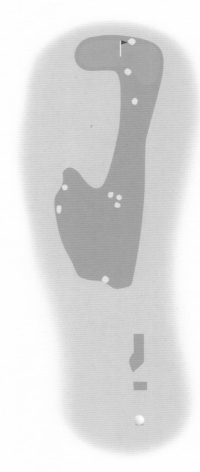

This relatively straightforward par 4 makes a welcome relief after the testing holes before it, and a brief respite before those holes that are still to come.

The 16th hole is one of the better strategic par 4s to play, and more of a challenge since it was extended in recent years. Once on the massive green—the largest at St. Andrews—you should contemplate two putts rather than going for glory.

Hole 17
ROAD

Distance: 455 yards / 416 meters

Par 4

Hole 18
TOM MORRIS

Distance: 357 yards / 326 meters

Par 4

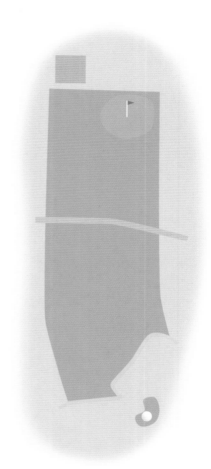

This treacherous par 4 is one of the best-loved holes in the world. Alterations made prior to the 2005 Open resulted in this hole becoming slightly more palatable, especially the refurbishment of the deadly bunker.

Named in honor of the four-time Open Champion and local golfer, Tom Morris is a tremendous hole to end your round. It offers the chance to finish with a flourish as you drive directly toward the historic clockface on the outside of the Royal & Ancient clubhouse.

GARY PLAYER COUNTRY CLUB (South Africa)

Gary Player Country Club, Sun City, North West Province, P.O. Box 6, Sun City 0316
www.suninternational.com

A world-renowned golf course, Sun City's Gary Player Country Club is a compelling par 72 course designed by South African golfing legend Gary Player. When played from the back tees it is one of the longest courses in the world, and since 1981 it has also been home to the annual Nedbank Golf Challenge—formerly known as the Million Dollar Challenge. The financially lucrative invitational event takes place every December, just as the international professional tours draw to a close, attracting many of the world's biggest

names to the state-of-the-art clubhouse and, of course, the chance of taking golf's largest financial prize—a cool US$1,200,000.

This flat course offers the ultimate in adventure golf, with stunning natural beauty complemented by spectacular water hazards, including an island green on the ninth hole. This testing course raises the bar even higher, with strategically-placed bunkers and cleverly hidden flagsticks on slick, kidney-shaped greens. Solid shots are vital to get past the hazards, although there are alternate tee locations available to make the course more manageable.

Great weather goes a long way to help promote this wonderfully conditioned golf course, which is open to the public all year round, except during and just before tournaments. The course is part of Sun International's mammoth resorts and borders the Lost City course—also designed by Player—as well as the Pilanesberg National Park.

Gary Player Country Club

Hole	1	2	3	4	5	6	7	8	9	10	11	12	13	14	15	16	17	18	Total
Par	4	5	4	3	4	4	3	4	5	5	4	3	4	5	4	3	4	4	72
Yards	441	569	449	213	491	424	225	492	596	547	458	219	444	601	471	211	478	502	7,832
Meters	403	520	411	195	449	388	206	450	545	500	419	200	406	550	431	193	437	459	7,162

Hole 1

Distance: 441 yards / 403 meters

Par 4

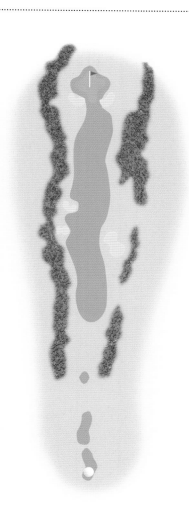

A straightforward hole to start a round, although nerves may set in at the sight of the recently introduced fairway bunker on the right, which is the main hazard to avoid.

Hole 2

Distance: 569 yards / 520 meters

Par 5

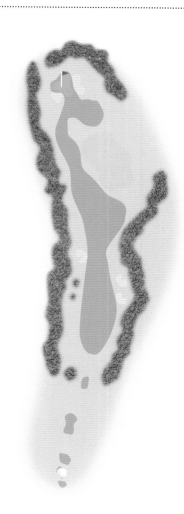

Recently lengthened because of the tendency of professionals to get birdies, many golfers will be tempted to try and land on the green in two shots. Accuracy from the tee determines whether there's the opportunity to achieve a birdie, which is still a possibility.

Hole 3

Distance: 449 yards / 411 meters

Par 4

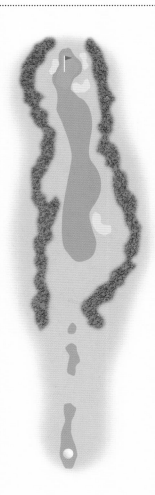

Hole 4

Distance: 213 yards / 195 meters

Par 3

A daunting hole because of the long layout and tiered green, this may be the toughest of the par 4 holes. It requires a well-hit tee shot to find safety from the heavy rough, with the green protected by bunkers on each side and more thick rough.

The first par 3 hole is not as easy as it appears, although a precise drive provides the opportunity for a birdie. The length of the hole is difficult to judge due to the downhill slope, and a short tee shot hit to the right will land in the water hazard of the large lake. Over-hitting leaves a tricky downhill putt for a birdie.

Hole 5

Distance: 491 yards / 449 meters

Par 4

Hole 6

Distance: 424 yards / 388 meters

Par 4

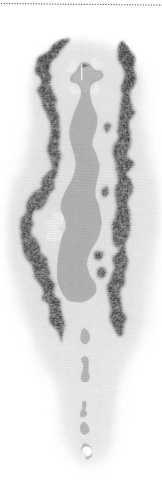

This hole was tweaked recently, as too many golfers got birdies. A new back tee increased the yardage and a bunker was introduced on the left of the fairway. However, after a successful drive, a long iron or wedge should give a great position on the well bunkered green.

As the shortest par 4, this is one of the most feasible birdie holes. A respectable drive is vital, as straying left of the fairway will result in a blind or oblique view of the green.

Hole 7

Distance: 225 yards / 206 meters

Par 3

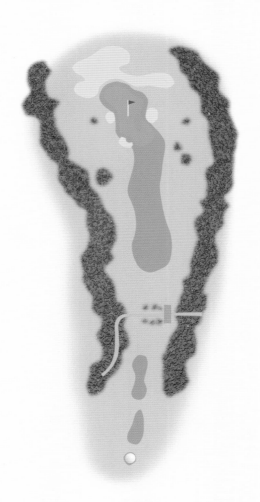

Hole 8

Distance: 492 yards / 450 meters

Par 4

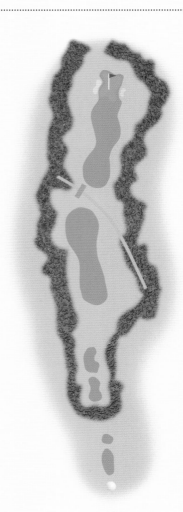

This deceptive hole needs to be handled with respect. It appears shorter than it is, enticing players with a seemingly feasible flagstick target. However, if the tee shot fades slightly to the left or right, players can expect to be penalized by the bunkers on the edge of the green.

Deadly accuracy is required for the opening two shots, otherwise a par or better is out of the question. This famously difficult hole features plenty of hazards, including dense bushes, plenty of rough, and a stream water hazard that crosses the fairway.

134

Hole 9

Distance: 596 yards / 545 meters

Par 5

Hole 10

Distance: 547 yards / 500 meters

Par 5

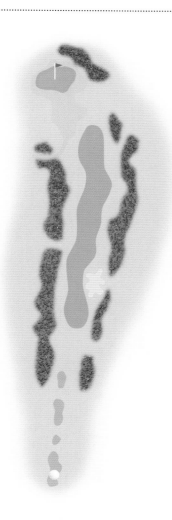

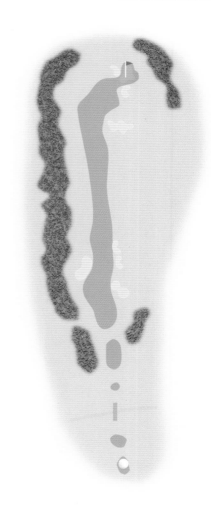

The course's signature hole is both daunting and dramatic, with an intimidating island green. It's easy to get into trouble, and any mishit shot is likely to be punished by the artificial rocks, bunkers, waterfalls, or water hazards.

Birdies or better are feasible for accurate big-hitters on this narrow par 5. However, long tee shots will do well to avoid any of the fairway bunkers, with a further three bunkers to miss before you get to the green.

Hole 11

Distance: 458 yards / 419 meters

Par 4

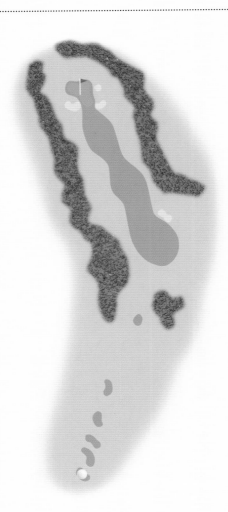

A powerful tee shot has to carry over a deep ravine in order to safely reach the fairway, and big-hitters will try to cut off as much of the angle of the dogleg as they can. The small, recently-introduced bunker adds menace to the fairway, with a tendency to trap over-hit drives and miss-hit second shots.

Hole 12

Distance: 219 yards / 200 meters

Par 3

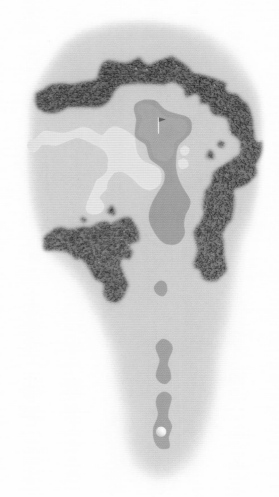

This deceptively short par 3 is played uphill, so plays longer than it appears. Over-hit shots will result in the ball rolling to the back of the slick and narrow green—and possibly into the rough—while shots that land short and left of the target will become trapped in the gigantic horseshoe-shaped bunker.

Hole 13

Distance: 444 yards / 406 meters

Par 4

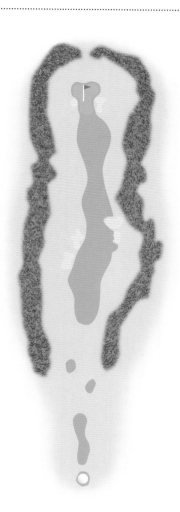

Hole 14

Distance: 601 yards / 550 meters

Par 5

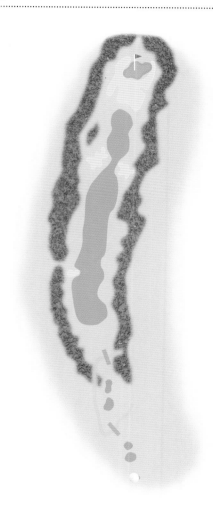

The tee shot is not for the nervous, as players face four fairway bunkers—two on each side. Accuracy is also needed to avoid the two small bunkers to either side of the green and the thick rough on the far right.

The longest hole on the course requires accuracy from the tee to lift the ball over the bushes and cut some of the distance off the obscured right side. A solid second shot is needed to get past the huge circular bunker, but over-hitting can put the ball in the punishing pampas grass surrounding the back of the green.

Hole 15

Distance: 471 yards / 431 meters

Par 4

Hole 16

Distance: 211 yards / 193 meters

Par 3

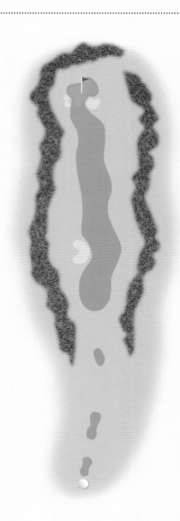

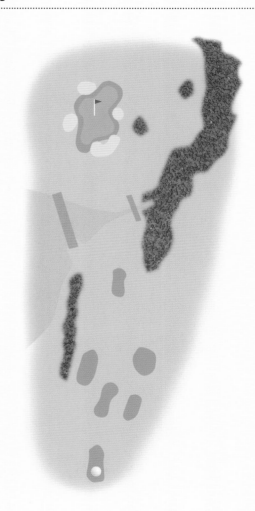

A straightforward-looking hole, and if the rough to the right of the fairway can be avoided there is a realistic chance of achieving a birdie on this short par 4.

This stunning downhill par 3 requires an accurate drive to reach the green, but it would take a serious mishit to end up in the large lake to the left of the fairway. The real hazards are the unforgiving bunkers—one at every corner of the green.

Hole 17

Distance: 478 yards / 437 meters

Par 4

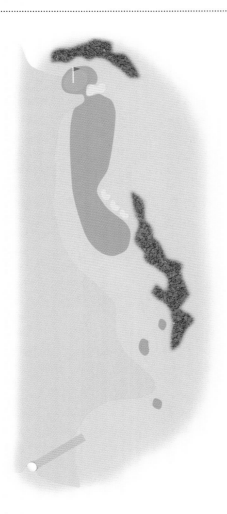

Hole 18

Distance: 502 yards / 459 meters

Par 4

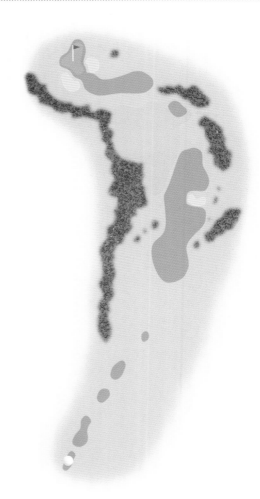

Recent reconstruction has seen this become a daunting proposition, with the emphasis on the player gambling with their shots. Should a tee shot be over-hit or pulled, the ball is likely to end up trapped in one of the three deep new bunkers, stuck in the bushes, or in the lake to the left of the fairway.

One of the toughest holes on the course, with a lake across the fairway and a recently introduced fairway bunker on the right. A long approach shot is needed to clear the lake and reach the small, undulating green, which is guarded by two bunkers. This demanding closing hole will penalize any minor mistakes.

ROYAL MELBOURNE GOLF CLUB, West Course (Australia)

Cheltenham Road, Black Rock, Victoria, 3193
www.royalmelbourne.com.au

Founded in 1891, the Royal Melbourne Golf Club is believed to be one of the oldest places to play golf in Australia, and four years after it opened it was granted royal status by Queen Victoria. However, the West Course at the current venue has only been in use since 1931, following its careful crafting by Dr. Alister MacKenzie. As a top designer, MacKenzie was highly sought after in the southern hemisphere, but made his only trip in 1926. His mission was to revamp the two links-style courses in Melbourne, namely the East and West courses tucked away in the historic Sand Belt in the Victoria region. He spent three months in the country, before leaving Alex Russell to supervise his instructions and recommendations alongside greenkeeper Mick Morcom.

Surprisingly, the rugged West course has no water hazards, with the superb challenge provided by tall grasses bordering wide fairways that lead to well-bunkered greens. From the tee there is plenty of margin for error on the huge fairways, and the natural rolling features mean that even miss-hit shots are likely to roll or ricochet back onto the fairways.

In stark contrast, the treacherous greens will lure unsuspecting golfers into making more putts than anticipated. Although the greens will be reached with few problems, the lethal combination of tricky contours, rock-hard firmness, and slick speed all place the emphasis on precision putting.

ROYAL MELBOURNE (West Course)

Hole	1	2	3	4	5	6	7	8	9	10	11	12	13	14	15	16	17	18	Total
Par	4	5	4	5	3	4	3	4	4	4	4	5	3	4	5	3	4	4	72
Yards	429	480	354	470	176	428	148	379	416	305	455	476	147	366	467	221	439	433	6,589
Meters	392	439	324	430	161	391	135	346	380	279	416	435	134	335	427	202	401	396	6,023

Hole 1

Distance: 429 yards / 392 meters

Par 4

Hole 2

Distance: 480 yards / 439 meters

Par 5

An accurate and powerful drive presents a genuine chance to start the round with a birdie, but straying off-center will be punished by a line of unplayable trees on the left or the deep bunker to the back and right of the fairway.

Another fantastic opportunity to hit a birdie—or better—on this straightforward par 5. The sloping green seems inviting from the fairway, but care is needed to avoid the heavy rough on the left and the deep bunkers on either side of the green.

Hole 3

Distance: 354 yards / 324 meters

Par 4

Hole 4

Distance: 470 yards / 430 meters

Par 5

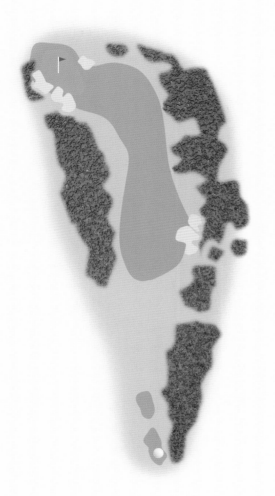

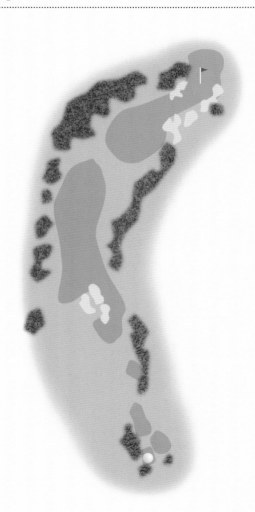

A deceptively short par 4 with a relatively large green, which can prove to be a hazardous trap as it slopes down the back. Bunkers guard both sides of the green, with those on the left particularly dangerous.

Hole 4 starts with a tough, but thrilling, uphill tee shot that is driven blindly onto the completely obscured fairway. Short shots will be punished by the bunkers, including perhaps the most challenging bunker in Australia at 15 feet (4.5 m) deep, with native shrubs and vegetation.

Hole 5

Distance: 176 yards / 161 meters

Par 3

Hole 6

Distance: 428 yards / 391 meters

Par 4

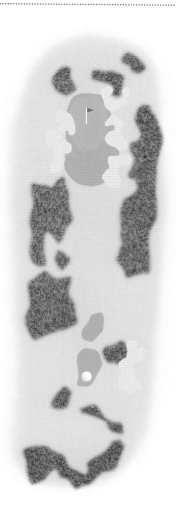

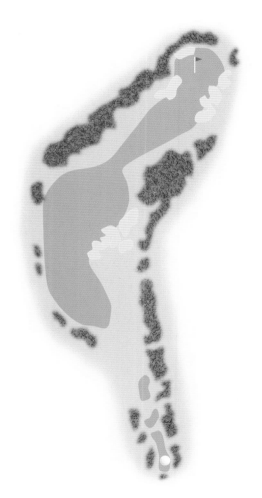

An outstanding, world-class, short par 3 with a striking similarity to the Eden hole at St. Andrews. The sloping green is heavily protected by a dune, covered by native Australian bushes and deep bunkers.

A visually striking and challenging dogleg par 4. It's important to judge the wind strength and direction before tackling the majestic sweeping fairway, dangerous corner bunkers, and what is possibly the most difficult green on the course.

Hole 7

Distance: 148 yards / 135 meters

Par 3

Hole 8

Distance: 379 yards / 346 meters

Par 4

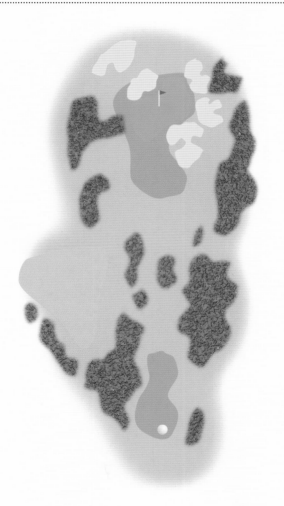

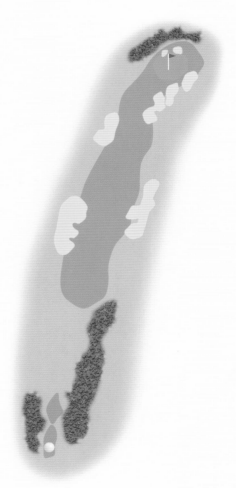

Built by golf course designer Ivo Whitton, this short par 3 requires pin-point accuracy. There are an array of hazards lying in wait for a mishit or misjudged drive, and an over-hit tee shot will be trapped by the difficult bunkers.

Another great chance to hit a birdie on this simple par 4, providing players miss the numerous bunkers guarding the front of the green, which itself slopes toward imposing back bunkers.

Hole 9

Distance: 416 yards / 380 meters

Par 4

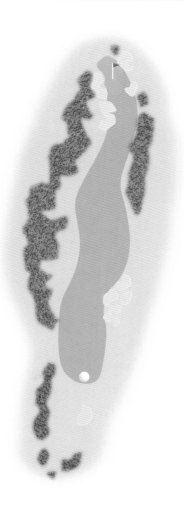

Hole 10

Distance: 305 yards / 279 meters

Par 4

This straightforward hole offers another chance of hitting a birdie. The green is well-protected by bunkers, with an especially treacherous bunker on the right to trap short shots.

Gambling on the uphill tee shot can result in a birdie or better on this short par 4. Big hitters will opt to try and bite off some of the dogleg on the left, but could land in severe trouble in the huge bunker.

Hole 15

Distance: 467 yards / 427 meters

Par 4

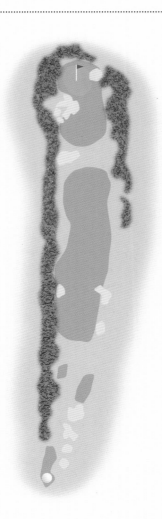

This par 4 was a longstanding joke started by golf course designer Dr. Alister MacKenzie, whose reaction to the hole's artificial mounding (now removed) was: "We shall leave it as is, to show future generations how silly golf course architecture used to be."

Hole 16

Distance: 221 yards / 202 meters

Par 3

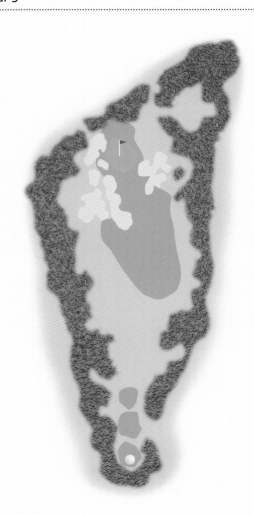

The last of four holes (13th to 16th) that are played in an adjoining property off the main boundaries of the golf course. The large bunkers hugging the entrance to the green require an accurate drive, aiming the ball away from the majority of hazards on the left.

148

Hole 17

Distance: 439 yards / 410 meters

Par 4

Hole 18

Distance: 433 yards / 396 meters

Par 4

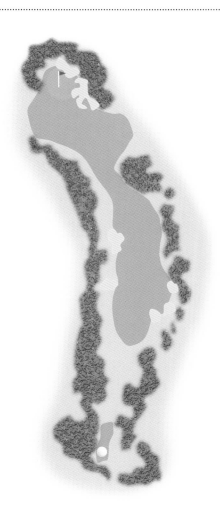

A complex dogleg par 4 with impressive bunkers surrounding the right side of the large green. There's the opportunity to hit a birdie if the green can be reached in two shots, but the huge bunkers provide a real danger.

The attractive closing hole is a revamped Dr. Alister MacKenzie masterpiece. The tee area and green have been moved and it requires a strong tee shot into the obscured dipping fairway. Faced with an uphill approach, wayward shots will be punished by the bunkers guarding the green.

ROYAL MELBOURNE GOLF CLUB, WEST COURSE (AUSTRALIA)

GLOSSARY

ACE
A hole-in-one stroke.

ADDRESS
Stance taken while preparing to hit the ball. The positioning of your body in relation to the golf ball.

AGGREGATE
Score made over more than one round of play, or by two or more players playing as partners.

AGGREGATE PLAY-OFF
When a series of holes are played until the winner of the tie is decided.

AIR SHOT
When a player misses the ball completely.

ALBATROSS
Former name of a "Double Eagle," which refers to the score for a hole made three strokes under par.

ALL SQUARE
Refers to a match where it is neck-and-neck, with no current overall leader.

ALTERNATE BALL
Players on a team alternate hitting each other's golf ball on every stroke until the hole is completed.

ALTERNATE SHOT
Golfers on a team take alternate shots, using the same ball or the best positioned golf ball depending on the match format

ANGLE OF APPROACH
Angle that the club moves upward or downward, toward the ball.

APPROACH PUTT
A long putt that is expected to finish close to the hole.

APPROACH SHOT
Shot played to the green.

APRON
Grassy area surrounding the green.

ATTACK
To play offensively and with purpose.

ATTEND THE FLAG
To hold and then remove the flag while another golfer attempts to putt their ball.

AWAY
The ball that's the greatest distance from the hole when more than one golfer is competing. The next ball to be played.

BACK DOOR
Rear of the hole.

BACK LIP
Edge of the bunker that lies furthest from the green.

BACK NINE
Second set of nine holes on an 18-hole course.

BACKSPIN
Reverse spin used to make the ball stop short on the green.

BACKSWING
Backward part of the player's swing, which starts from the ground and goes back over the head.

BAIL OUT
To avoid direct hazards by hitting the ball toward a different area of the hole.

BALATA
Resilient, sap-like substance from the South American Balata tree used to make a cover for rubber-cored golf balls.

BALL AT REST
When your ball has come to a halt after being hit.

BALL HOLED
The ball has to be entirely below the lip of the hole to be deemed "holed."

BALL IN PLAY
Once a golfer has made a shot, or attempted to hit the ball, it is "in play" until it is holed out or unplayable.

BALL MARKER
Used to spot the position of the ball on the green prior to lifting it.

BALL MARK REPAIR TOOL
Fork-shaped tool used to fix marks made by the ball landing on the green.

BANANA BALL
An extreme sliced shot that curves to the right in the shape of a banana.

BASEBALL GRIP
Holding the club with all 10 fingers on the grip.

BEND
Curve created by sidespin on a shot.

BENT GRASS
A resilient type of grass used on courses that can be cut extremely short.

BERMUDA
Very smooth type of grass, mostly used in North America.

BEST BALL
Played in teams of two, three, or four. Each golfer in a team plays their shots using their own ball, with the lowest individual score in a team (the "best ball") counted as the team score. The lowest score overall wins the hole.

BETTER BALL
Refers to a Match Play or Stroke Play competition when two players on the same team each play the "better" positioned ball.

BINGO-BANGO-BONGO
Competition format played by individuals. After the first stroke, shots are taken in the order of who is furthest away from the hole. Three points are available to win on every hole, with the winner being the player with the highest score overall. A point is awarded for: the first ball to reach the green; the closest to the hole once all balls are on the green; the first golfer to hole their putt.

BIRDIE
One stroke under par for a hole.

BIRD'S NEST
Refers to a ball when it is cupped in deep grass.

BITE
The backspin put on the ball to stop it dead, with little or no roll.

BLADE
Striking part of an iron clubhead.

BLADE PUTTER
Type of putter with an iron head that maintains the same basic format as standard numbered irons.

BLIND BOGEY
Competition format where golfers attempt to score closest to a number drawn at random.

BLIND HOLE
Refers to an unsighted green for a golfer on their approach shot.

BLOCK
Playing a shot by delaying the rotation of the wrists during a swing.

BOGEY
One over par score for the hole.

BOGEY COMPETITION
Stroke Play format where golfers play against a fixed score on every hole.

BOGEY GOLFERS
Players with a handicap of 20.

BOGEY RATING
The difficulty of a course under normal course and weather conditions for a bogey golfer. The bogey rating is a graded number that is used in the formula for calculating slope ratings.

BOUNDARY
Edge of the golf course that indicates the legitimate area of play.

BREAK
i) The way that the ball will bounce or roll.
ii) The sideways slope of the green.

BUNKER
Hazard, usually comprising of sand in bare ground.

BUNT
An intentional short shot.

BURIED BALL
Ball that is partially beneath the sand in a bunker.

CADDIE (CADDY)
Person who transports a player's clubs during play and offers him assistance in accordance with the Rules.

CALLAWAY
Competition format played by individuals where golfers do not have a verifiable (or very high) handicap. This format should even out all the scores in a consistent and fair manner.

CARRY
The distance the ball travels after it first hits the ground.

CASUAL WATER
Temporary accumulation of water that is not a water hazard, such as a puddle.

CHAPMAN PINEHURST
Played by teams of two players. Strokes are individually taken by each golfer, with the balls switched between team members for the second shot. From the third shot onward, the better ball is chosen and the golfers play alternate shots until the hole is completed.

CHIP SHOT
Short approach shot of low trajectory, usually used to reach the green from the fairway.

CHIP-IN
Chip shot that is holed.

CHOKE
To grip further down on the club handle.

CHOP
Hacking motion used to hit the ball.

CLEAT
The spike on the sole of a golf shoe.

CLOSED FACE
When the clubface points to the left of the target as you address the ball.

CLOSED OUT
Refers to the completion of a match using the Match Play format, when a team is "up" (leading) and there are fewer holes remaining than the number of holes behind. A point is awarded when the match is "closed out."

CLOSED STANCE
Stance with the right foot pulled back and away from the ball.

CLUBHEAD
Striking area of the club.

CLUBHOUSE
Main building on the course where business matters are undertaken.

HOOK
To hit the ball in a manner that causes it to curve from right to left for right-handed players—or vice-versa for left-handed golfers.

HOSEL
Hollow part of an iron clubhead in which the shaft is fitted.

IMPACT
Refers to the exact moment when the club strikes the ball.

IN
The second set of nine holes on an 18-hole course. Also known as the "Back nine"

INSIDE
Being nearer the hole than your opponent.

INTERLOCKING GRIP
Type of grip where the little finger of the left hand is intertwined with the index finger of the right hand, for a right handed player. Vice-versa applies to a left-handed golfer.

INTENDED LINE
Line you expect the ball to travel after you have hit it.

IRON
Clubs with a head made of iron or steel.

KICK
Refers to an erratic bounce.

KILL THE BALL
Refers to hitting a long shot.

LAG
Refers to leaving your putt close to the hole to ensure that you will hole it on your next shot.

LATERAL HAZARD
Any hazard running parallel to the line of play.

LAY UP
To play a safer and shorter shot than normally might be attempted.

LIE
The position in which the ball rests on the ground.

LINE
The correct path played toward the green, whether putting or on the fairway.

LINE UP
The study of the green to determine how to hit your putt.

LINKS
Refers to any golf course, although originally referred only to courses next to a beach.

LIP
Top rim of the hole.

LOB SHOT
Stroke that goes straight up and comes virtually straight down with little spin.

LOCAL RULES
Set of rules for a club determined by the members.

LOFT
Refers to the elevation of the ball in the air.

LONG GAME
Refers to shots hit with high-irons and the woods.

LOOSE IMPEDIMENTS
Any natural object that is not fixed or growing.

LOW-IRONS
Iron clubs that are used to generate distance, such as a 1-iron, 2-iron, or 3-iron.

MALLET
Putter with a wider and heavier head than a conventional blade putter.

MARKER
A small object used to mark the spot of the ball when it is lifted off the green.

MARKERS
Objects placed at the teeing area that indicate the area for golfers to play their drives from.

MASHIE-IRON
Another name for the No.4 iron.

MASHIE-NIBLICK
Another name for the No.6 iron.

MATCH PLAY
Competition format where each hole is a separate contest. The original form of golf competition.

MEDALIST
The player with the lowest qualifying score in a tournament.

MEDAL PLAY
Competition decided by the overall number of strokes used to complete the round(s).

MID-IRONS
Refers to iron clubs that are used to find a happy medium in terms of accuracy and distance, such as a 5-iron or 6-iron.

MODIFIED STAPLEFORD
Played as individuals and in teams. A stroke index is determined for each hole, with the number of shots allowed for golfers per hole dependent on their individual handicaps and the hole's stroke index. To calculate the score, the lowest number of shots is deducted from the expected number of shots. The highest score at the end of the match wins.

NECK
Tapered projecting part where the shaft of the club joins the head.

NET SCORE
Player's final score after he deducts his handicap.

NINETEENTH HOLE
Refers to the clubhouse bar.

OBSTRUCTION
Artificial object that has been left or placed on the course. Does not include boundary markers.

OFFSET
Club with the head set behind the shaft.

ON PAR
Refers to scoring level par for an individual hole.

ONE POINT
Awarded for each match won by a team.

ONE UP
Having scored one hole more than your opponent in Match Play.

OPEN STANCE
When one foot is dropped behind the imaginary line of the direction of the ball.

OUT
The inaugural nine holes of an 18-hole course.

OUT OF BOUNDS
Area outside the course where play is prohibited.

OUTSIDE AGENCY
Anyone who is not part of the competitor's side in Stroke Play.

OVERLAPPING GRIP
Having the little finger of the right hand overlapping the space between the forefinger and second finger of the left hand, for right-handed players. Vice-versa for left-handed golfers.

PAIRS
Two golfers playing together in a stroke competition.

PAIRINGS
Refers to groups of two players.

PAR
The number of shots a golfer should take to complete a hole or round with good performance.

PARKLAND
Course laid out in grassland with little rough.

PEG
The tee.

PEORIA SYSTEM
Competition format played by individuals, which is suited to golfers without handicaps, or with a high handicap. Golfers earn points at the end of the round, which modifies their score to give a revised total.

PERSIMMON
Wood with a distinctive grain.

PICK UP
To take up one's ball before holing out. In Match Play this means the hole has been conceded and in Stroke Play this leads to disqualification.

PIN
Another name for the flagstick.

PINEHURST
Competition format variation in which a golfer plays their partner's drive, with one ball picked to finish the hole.

PITCH
Short shot lofting the ball into the air in a high arc and landing with backspin.

PITCHING IRONS
Refers to the high-irons, such as the 7-iron, 8-iron, and 9-iron.

PITCHING WEDGE
Iron club designed for making pitch shots.

PLACEMENT
Accuracy in the targeting of a shot.

PLAYING THROUGH
Passing another group of players who are slowly playing ahead.

PLUS GOLFERS
Golfers with a handicap of less than zero. Their handicap is added to the score, rather than deducted.

POT BUNKER
Small, deep sand trap with steep sides.

PRACTICE GREEN
Green set up for putting practice.

PREFERRED LIE
A local rule that allows golfers to improve their lie in a specific manner, without penalty.

PROVISIONAL BALL
A ball played if the original ball is believed to be out of bounds or lost.

PULL
A ball that goes to the left of the target with little curve as hit by a right-handed golfer. Vice-versa for left-handed players.

PUNCH
Low, controlled shot into the wind, hit by a short swing.

PUSH
Ball that goes to the right of the target with very little curving for a right-handed golfer. Vice-versa for left-handed players.

PUTT
The shot made on the putting green, which derives from a Scottish term meaning "to nudge."

155

PUTT OUT
To hole the ball with a putt.

PUTTER
Short-shafted club with a straight face to make putting easy.

PUTTING GREEN
Surface area around the hole that is especially trimmed for putting.

R&A
Royal & Ancient Golf Club of St. Andrews, Fife, Scotland. Producer of the official *Rules of Golf*.

READING THE GREEN
Analyzing the contour and texture of the path that the ball will take on its way to the hole.

RECOVER
To play the ball back into a satisfactory position on the course.

REVERSE OVERLAP
A putting grip in which the index finger of the right hand overlaps the little finger of the left for right-handed golfers, and vice-versa for left-handed players.

RIM
To run the ball round the edge of the cup of the hole.

RIM OUT
To run around the edge of the cup and fail to fall in.

ROUGH
Long grass areas adjacent to fairway, greens, tee areas, or hazards.

ROUND
A complete game of golf, with 18 holes referred to as one round.

RUB OF THE GREEN
Any accident, not caused by a player or caddie, that moves or stops a ball in play and for which no relief is given.

RUN
The distance the ball rolls when it lands on the ground.

RUN-UP
Approach shot that is close to the ground, or on the ground.

SAND TRAP
Another name for a bunker.

SAND WEDGE
An iron with a heavy flange on the bottom, designed for escaping from bunkers.

SCRAMBLE
Team competition played in teams of two, three, or four, where golfers play the best ball of a team member after every stroke or drive. Variations exist, such as Ambrose Scramble (individual handicaps are used to calculate the final score), Florida Scramble (the golfer whose shot was selected as the best is not permitted to play the next shot), and Texas Scramble (each golfer must play at least four tee shots).

SCRATCH PLAYER
Refers to a player who has a handicap of zero.

SET UP
To position yourself for the address of the ball.

SHAFT
The part of the club joined to the head.

SHANK
A shot struck by the club's hosel that travels to the right of the intended target.

SHORT GAME
The part of the game that is made up of chip shots, pitching and putting.

SKY
To hit underneath the ball and send it higher than intended.

SLICE
A shot that curves strongly from left to right as a result of sidespin for right-handed golfers, and vice-versa for left-handed players.

SLOPE
Adjusts your handicap to the difficulty of the course you play. The more difficult the course, the more strokes you'll need.

SOLE
The base of the clubhead.

SPRAY
To hit the ball erratically off line.

SQUARE STANCE
The placing of a golfer's feet in a line parallel to the direction that the ball will travel in.

STABLEFORD
Method of scoring using points instead of strokes. Competition format played by individuals and teams in either alternating shot, best ball, or scramble formats.

STANCE
The position of a player's feet when addressing the ball.

STARTER
The person who determines the order of play from the first tee.

STRAIGHT-FACED
Refers to a club with little loft on the face.

STRIKE OFF
To drive the ball from the tee area.

STROKE
The forward motion of the clubhead made with the intent to hit the ball, whether or not contact is made.

STROKE PLAY
A competition where the total number of strokes for one round, or an agreed number of rounds, determines the winner.

STYMIE
Originally used to describe an opponent's ball lying in the line of another player's putt, but in recent years refers to any object in the way of a shot.

SUDDEN DEATH PLAY-OFF
Refers to holes being played until the tie is decided.

SWALE
A moderately contoured depression or dip in the terrain.

SWING
The physical action of hitting the ball.

TAKEAWAY
The start of the backswing.

TEE AREA
The position from where the ball is hit on the first shot of the hole.

TEE
i) A disposable device, normally a plastic or wooden peg, on which the ball is placed for driving.
ii) An abbreviation for the tee area.

TEE OFF
To play a tee shot.

TEE UP
To begin play by placing the ball on the tee.

TEE-SHOT
A shot played from a tee.

TEEING GROUND
The area in which you must tee off your ball. The ball must be teed off within the markers, and no more than two club lengths behind them.

THIN
The ball is hit thin when it is hit above center with the clubhead, traveling on too high a line.

THREE BALL
Three golfers playing against each other, each playing their own ball.

THREESOME
A match in which two players play the same ball and alternate strokes, and play against a single player. Also means three players playing a round of golf together.

TOP
To hit the ball above its center, causing it to roll instead of rising.

TOPSPIN
Forward rotation of the ball in motion.

TOUCH
The accuracy—especially in putting—of how the ball is placed.

TOUCH SHOT
A delicately hit shot.

TRAJECTORY
Flight path of the ball.

TRIPLE BOGEY
A score of three over par on an individual hole.

UNDERSPIN
Reverse spin used to make the ball stop short on the green.

UNPLAYABLE LIE
A lie in which the ball is impossible to play out of.

UP
Refers to the difference in the number of holes won and also the specified number of strokes that you are ahead of your opponent in Match Play.

UPRIGHT SWING
A swing that carries the clubhead more directly backward and upward from the ball.

USGA
United States Golf Association.

VARDON GRIP
An overlapping grip.

WEDGE
An iron with a high loft that is used for short shots.

WHIFF
To swing and miss the ball completely.

WOOD
A club, which can be made of metal or wood, that has a large head and is used for hitting shots over a long distance.

X
The symbol written on a scorecard when a player fails to complete a hole or is otherwise unable to write down a stroke score.

YARDAGE RATING
Difficulty of a hole, based on its yardage.

157

INDEX

158

159

I lovingly dedicate this book to
my late great-uncle, Douglas Hale,
whose unwavering passion for
the great game inspired me.

God bless him.

**"When he comes to the Great
Game, he must go alone—
alone, and at peril of his head."**

Rudyard Kipling